Applications of ICT in Social Scie...

Biljana Mileva Boshkoska (ed.)

Applications of ICT in Social Sciences

Bibliographic Information published by the Deutsche Nationalbibliothek
The Deutsche Nationalbibliothek lists this publication in the Deutsche Nationalbibliografie; detailed bibliographic data is available in the internet at http://dnb.d-nb.de.

Library of Congress Cataloging-in-Publication Data

Applications of ICT in social sciences / Biljana Mileva Boshkoska (ed.).
    pages cm
  ISBN 978-3-631-66017-1
  1. Information technology--Social aspects. 2. Social sciences--Research. I.
Boshkoska, Biljana Mileva, 1979-
  HM851.A728 2015
  300.72--dc23
                        2014048385

ISBN 978-3-631-66017-1 (Print)
E-ISBN 978-3-653-05304-3 (E-Book)
DOI 10.3726/978-3-653-05304-3

© Peter Lang GmbH
Internationaler Verlag der Wissenschaften
Frankfurt am Main 2015
All rights reserved.
PL Academic Research is an Imprint of Peter Lang GmbH.

Peter Lang – Frankfurt am Main · Bern · Bruxelles · New York ·
Oxford · Warszawa · Wien

This publication has been peer reviewed.

www.peterlang.com

Acknowledgments

This publication is funded by the Creative Core FISNM-3330-13-500033 'Simulations' project funded by the European Union, the European Regional Development Fund. The operation is carried out within the framework of the Operational Programme for Strengthening Regional Development Potentials for the period 2007–2013, Development Priority 1: Competitiveness and Research Excellence, Priority Guideline 1.1: Improving the Competitive Skills and Research Excellence.

**Fakulteta za
informacijske študije**
Faculty of information studies

Kreativno jedro:
Simulacije
Creative core: Simulations

»Operacijo delno financira Evropska unija in sicer iz Evropskega sklada za regionalni razvoj. Operacija se izvaja v okviru Operativnega programa krepitve regionalnih razvojnih potencialov za obdobje 2007–2013, 1. razvojne prioritete: Konkurenčnost podjetij in raziskovalna odličnost, prednostne usmeritve 1.1: Izboljšanje konkurenčnih sposobnosti podjetij in raziskovalna odličnost.«

"The operation is partially financed by the European Union, mostly from the European Regional Development Fund. Operation is performed in the context of the Operational program for the strengthening regional development potentials for the period 2007–2013, 1st development priorities: Competitiveness of the companies and research excellence, priority aim 1.1: Improvement of the competitive capabilities of the companies and research excellence."

REPUBLIKA SLOVENIJA
**MINISTRSTVO ZA IZOBRAŽEVANJE,
ZNANOST IN ŠPORT**

Naložba v vašo prihodnost
OPERACIJO DELNO FINANCIRA EVROPSKA UNIJA
Evropski sklad za regionalni razvoj

Contents

Preface

The usage of information and communication technologies (ICT) in the field of social sciences is a growing phenomenon, emanating from today's need for knowledge about society and the economy, and as a result we are striving to create ideas and methods for the better use of information. This book includes some of the latest practices from business process management and modelling to relationship marketing. Covering a variety of examples taken from real life, such as education, web clipping, public safety, tactic knowledge, and the protection of intellectual property, this book outlines state-of-the-art social sciences applications and their implementation with ICT.

Nadja Damij and Jernej Agrež
Faculty of Information Studies in Novo mesto, Slovenia

Social Media Knowledge Influence on a Loosely Coupled System: A Case Study of an Informal Humanitarian Initiative

Abstract: Notwithstanding that in Slovenia there is no conceptual solution that would integrate social media within formal emergency operating procedures, social media has become a tool for supporting official responses during emergencies. In this chapter, we introduce a conceptual optimization of natural disaster standard operating procedures, which reveals points at which it is possible to integrate social media with the formal response process. We take as a case study the ice storm that affected Slovenia in the beginning of 2014, which, because of the downfall of communication lines and the electrical power grid, caused the isolation of the whole region. Running in parallel with the official response, social media enabled emerging of informal loosely coupled initiatives that reacted to the humanitarian aid and the call for power generators. The efficiency of the social media-based response was high, and successfully complemented official activities. This is the first optimization approach of this kind in Slovenia, and we expect it to serve as a base ground for further research on the connection between social media and emergency management.

Keywords: Social media, knowledge influence, loosely coupled systems, natural disasters

1 Introduction

The prevalence and global reach of social media enables a viral spread of published information in audio visual, graphic or textual form. Woerndl et al. (2008, p. 34) argues that social media constitutes a core infrastructure for viral spread, supported by peer to peer interaction that selector-specifies message targets and avoids transmission dead-ends. It provides online users with tools that make information sharing virtually effortless, contributing to viral share by "encouraging the user to share feedback, provide comments, rate products, provide reviews and download item[s] for sharing with friends" (Gilfoil 2012, p. 70). Viral information spread allows decision-makers who work in a specific field to obtain important information about that field almost immediately after the information has been published. Similar to the phenomena of social influence, whereby "individuals' behaviors or opinions are affected by their social environment" (Xia & Liu 2013, p. 1), important information will affect the decision taken, just as it would in the case of a specific decision-maker intentionally using social media as an information source. When decisions are urgent, with high and diverse stakes, with considerable uncertainty and ignorance involved, and when trust is fragile, "decision-making needs to be understood as a process with multiple sources of information and research evidence" (Grossberndt 2012, p. 2), and social media nowadays represents an important information and knowledge source. While the worldwide reach of social media on the one hand increases the information pool for an individual decision-maker, on the other hand, it involves a crowd becoming a constantly present, yet loosely organized, decision support mechanism. "To make crowdsourcing work, there is a basic requirement to make external parties aware of the challenges or problems that need to be solved. Various digital marketing tools, especially social media platforms, provide new ways to foster the interaction between the parties" (Simula, Töllinen & Karjaluoto 2013, p. 122).

Not only has that involvement of the crowd through social media become unavoidable, but the crowd gets channeled onto the specifically designed crowdsourcing platforms that provide it with the ability to create its own contribution. "The concept of organizations as loosely coupled systems is widely used and diversely understood" (Orton & Weick 1990, p. 203). Glassman (1973, p. 83) set the definition of loose coupling as interaction among activities shared between two systems with the condition that there are only few such activities, or that they are weak when compared to the others within the system. Further, Weick (1976, p. 2) describes a loosely coupled system as an organization in which entities connect with weak links which allow them to retain their own identity and separateness. Principles of loosely coupled systems can be identified in a wide range of organizational practices. Frandsen, Morsing and Vallentin (2013, p. 238) presented a loosely coupled approach for sustainability adoption; Moilanen (2011, p. 138) found that loose coupling as a managerial tool may stimulate generative organizational learning. The question arises of how such systems perform when triggered by emergency events relating to public safety or homeland security issues. Koven (2010, p. 353) criticized official public and private response during hurricane Katrina, even though Busch and Givens (2012, p. 16) found public–private cooperation an important factor that strengthens national resilience. Holguín-Veras et al. (2012, p. 15) identified similar deficiencies in response during catastrophic events such as hurricane Katrina, the earthquake in Haiti and the tsunami that affected Fukushima, arguing that the most difficult part of the necessary solution was to integrate all segments of affected society into the response. A similar discovery was made by O'Brien et al. (2010, p. 504), but emphasizing community and social learning to support resilience building. Even though many authors have researched loosely coupled systems, the problem of how knowledge interaction within such system influences process patterns has not been studied to its full extent.

In this chapter, we present the influences and contributions of social media and the following consequential phenomena: information spread, communication, fieldwork coordination and crowdsourcing in the context of disaster management and standard operating procedures, using workflow diagrams. The case that we analyzed dates from the beginning of 2014, when the ice storm hit most of Slovenia and heavily affected the Notranjska region. We determined the importance of social media within the response process of the loosely coupled response initiatives that took place 150 km away in the Posavje region, which felt minimal consequences from the storm. We used the method of observation in order to follow the response process from the widest possible perspective. Further on, we conducted semi-structured interviews with key entities that were active within the initiatives and also gathered information about the temporal dynamic of the social media activities that are available online on the social networks that were used during the response. We used a process modelling method to construct a workflow diagram of response initiatives and additionally developed a knowledge map that reveals the influences of social media in the response process. For modelling we used the additional knowledge module, developed for process-knowledge interaction indication on the basis of "TAD methodology" (Damij 2000, p. 23).

The contribution of this research is presented within the graphic optimi-zation model that provides us with insight as to what potential there is to include social media, and the crowd that is using its services daily, in the standard operating procedures of the national disaster protection system and how such inclusion could increase the efficiency of the formal response process.

2 Method

For the purpose of this paper, we conducted a literature review to be able to determine the state of existing knowledge. We collected data, used in the research through the observation method, where we recorded all necessary aspects of the research object. We also gathered information from the online media portals and social networks. Further, we used a business process management simulation environment to create a response process model, which served as a base structure for building a knowledge map. Using the same concept, we developed a process optimization of a national standard operating procedure.

3 Influential Incident Information

Depending on the source and magnitude of the incident, local emergency informing and alert mechanisms together with local media will be the earliest sources to provide gathered and processed information to the public. Nevertheless, these sources will not be the only or the very first, neither will they affect the wider community as significantly as the content spread through social media. A report by the Slovenian Environment Agency about the ice storm between January 30 and February 3, 2014, reveals that an early warning was issued on January 30 at 9am and an additional warning that forecasted heavy snow storms was issued at 6:30pm. On January 31 the media began covering the sensational weather phenomenon and its consequences, with titles such as: "Snow Causes Truck Accidents and Chaos on the Roads"; "After the Snow, Rain and Slipperiness"; "Trees on Railways Cause Delays"; "Weather Will Hinder Any Movement"; "I Wanted to Cry"; "Emergency in Pivka: Children in Schools without Electricity and Heating"; "Helpless: You Cannot Enter the car, Nor Control It"; and "Meteorologists: This Is Not the Usual Weather". Even though meteorological alerts were issued and the media covered the news promptly, the daily emergency response reports of the Administration for Civil Protection and Disaster Relief for January 30 to January 31 reveal that people in the affected regions were not fully aware or prepared for the oncoming disaster. Reports (URSZR SPIN, 2014) reveal that 27 car accidents occurred in 24 hours due to adverse weather conditions and that there were more than 40 technical interventions caused by an underestimation of the weather conditions.

Higher awareness of the seriousness of the situation came with the spread of the graphic and audiovisual content published online by individual social network users. Citizens of the most affected region began taking and publishing visuals of the landscape captured in ice. Local media which usually focused its reach on a regional level had first-hand information on the ice severity and began publishing the information through social media, causing its spread nationwide. It was not until February 2 that, through their web portals, larger media companies first brought attention to the situation. Topics like "Red Alert for Slovenia, No Classes for 75 % of Schools, 80.000 Households without Electricity" were highlighted on the morning news, and less affected Slovenian regions slowly got a realistic impression what was happening in the Notranjska region.

February 2 is also the date on which the Administration for Civil Protection and Disaster Relief published its first briefing on the situation in Notranjska region and issued instructions on how to react during the emergency. From January 31 until February 2, social media allowed the viral spread of influential information that consequently triggered an unofficial response of the crowd. In the crucial moments when other means of communications (including the national emergency system of radio communications) failed due to the breakdown of the electricity network, social media became the only communication channel that allowed communication among individuals and organizations.

4 The Emergence of Loosely Coupled Initiatives due to Social Media Intervention

In the case of the ice storm and the consequences that followed we easily distinguish between formal and informal responses; formal separates local action conducted by local government from regional action that is organized and implemented by the national government's Administration for Civil Protection and Disaster Relief. At the time of ice storm neither at local level nor at regional level was there a standard operating procedure that would deliver instructions how to respond and what to expect. In order to deploy the civil protection force, the Administration activated its standard operating procedure for protection against flooding. This did not predict the possible consequences of the ice storm, causing inattention to and isolation of the households on higher terrain and leaving citizens without proper information about the ongoing situation. After the first information wave that brought insights into the level of the devastation, social media continued to deliver another set of information from the region. These concerned the low efficiency of the formal response on the local level, short reports about isolated households and broken communication, and facts indicating affected food and fresh water supply and families that were consequently unable to prepare their daily food. First among the local organizations that decided to take action even though they were not officially part of disaster protection system was the Scouting group Rod Kraških Viharnikov. They established a crisis center in Postojna that became the main provider of food, hot drinks, information and shelter in the town of Postojna.

However, it was not only in the Notranjska region that individuals and organizations had a self-organized response. Initiatives also started to form in other regions of Slovenia, including the region of Posavje. Figure 1 summarizes the progression of activities conducted by loosely coupled initiatives in the Posavje region. Following the information on social media and other conventional sources, the first initiative arose at a school in the town of Brežice. Using Facebook and internal information sharing, Gymnasium Brežice managed to provide accommodation for those students and their families from the affected towns. Even though the families were in need of proper accommodation, Gymnasium's initiative was politely put on hold by those official organizations that had the competence to respond, due to broken communication with the students. The same social media posts reached the president of the rescue dog society in the town of Brežice. Rescue Responders had already begun posting notices about collecting food, water and other urgent supplies for the affected region on several social media profiles. These were based on the newly opened Facebook profile of Postojna crisis center, which announced its establishment and launched the very first call in the region for humanitarian aid and additional volunteer support. Using only social media information sharing, Rescue Responders immediately received four offers for a location in the towns of Brežice and Krško from which to organize the collecting of humanitarian aid. Having the logistics network covered, they began spreading information about collection points, to prevent saturation of storage places and to shorten travel for those people who intended to bring humanitarian aid.

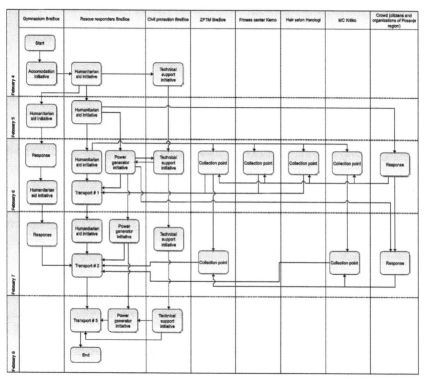

Fig. 1: Workflow diagram of a loosely coupled initiative

Based on social media posts and photos by the Postojna crisis center and members of local fire brigades, who shared information that they were getting ready for deployment, Rescue Responders made contact with the deputy commander of the local civil protection force in order to negotiate an official response with the civil protection technical support team. At the time, the deputy commander had no intention to deploy the team, but when he got a notice about initiatives going on he made emergency contact with the Mayor of the Brežice municipality and gave the local civil protection force permission to deploy a technical support team to the affected region in three days' time. Special transport was organized to deliver civil protection members, Rescue Responders, other individuals and their equipment to Logatec, where they assisted in cleaning a riverbed that was filled with broken trees and waste wood, threatening nearby houses with possible flooding.

Social media information sharing brought collection point information back to the affected region and triggered the first cooperative feedback. At the same time, rescue dog responders from Brežice organized humanitarian aid collections in the town of Logatec, one of the most affected places, and another rescue dog society organized local support to those families who, after 5 days, remained off the electricity grid. The president of the Logatec Rescue Responders reacted to the Brežice initiative, posting a Facebook comment that households in Logatec urgently needed power generators for people to be able to cook their food, take a shower, and run those central heating systems that were unable to run without electricity. Having difficulties with cellphone communication because of the heavily damaged infrastructure, societies used Facebook private chat to arrange a two-day response action plan that led to a new collecting priority—power generators—and two final delivery locations for collected aid, the crisis center in Postojna and a local fire station in Logatec.

By the time the first transport arrived at the Postojna crisis center and Postojna fire brigade station, the social media information boost focusing on power generators had already reached the first individuals who were willing to lend their generators to those people in the affected region. Information spread even reached older people; while many of them do not use social media, their younger relatives do. At the same time, a medium-sized corporation provided five stronger power generators, and a regional student organization lent their electricity installation cables and hubs, usually used for supplying bigger events with enough electrical power. The power hardware, additional food and other aid gathered at collection points was delivered to Logatec and Postojna with the second transport.

5 Social Media, Information Sharing, Decision-Making, Crowdsourcing

Social media played a key role as an information distribution channel that affected decision-making within loosely coupled initiatives. In order to be able to follow information flow and the creation of the knowledge that served as a basis on which decisions were taken, we built the knowledge map presented in Figure 2. The knowledge map upgrades the process diagram with additional knowledge and information sources that were not directly involved in activities within the process, but influenced the initiatives through information and knowledge sharing. Additionally, the map gives us insight into the activities and entities where new knowledge emerged (knowledge locations), activities and entities that contributed to the information shared (information locations) and links between different knowledge and information locations.

We identified five knowledge locations, among which one (entity: Civil Protection Brežice; activity: technical support initiative) had not received any information input from social media and will be excluded from further analysis. The remaining knowledge locations were distributed between two entities: Gymnasium Brežice and Rescue Responders Brežice. The highest decision weight location was at Rescue Responders Brežice, whose activity was the humanitarian aid initiative. Decisions taken under the influence of this knowledge location mark the event horizon of all following initiatives and their activities within the response. Information input to the location was delivered only through social media channels, creating knowledge that triggered the decision to begin the response. The knowledge location at Gymnasium Brežice was an important, but not crucial influence. We can label it as an accelerator that contributed to faster sharing of the information about the inefficient response of the official responsible services. Two knowledge locations bound to an entity, Rescue Responders Brežice, influenced two additional decisions. The first knowledge location within the activity, the power generator initiative, shifted focus from collecting mostly humanitarian aid to a new priority: to collect as many power generators as possible to transport to the affected region. The second and knowledge location within the activity, the first transport initiative, influenced the decision to organize further transports to the affected region.

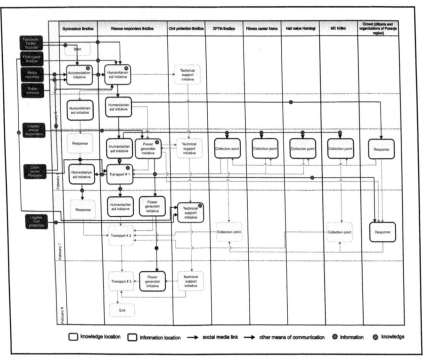

Fig. 2: Knowledge map

All of the above-described decision locations were mostly influenced by the information shared through social media, while social media was the only input to the informal response. Collection points were activated by the input of information to social media and this information was redistributed through social networks, creating crowdsourcing activity dynamics that were reflected in high amount of collected humanitarian aid and a high number of collected power generators.

Several types of crowdsourcing or activities similar to crowdsourcing developed or merged with the activities of informal initiatives during the response process. Initial crowdsourcing developed spontaneously from the information demand–supply dynamic. It caused a viral information spread that in a short time period covered all geographic regions of Slovenia and informed people countrywide about the ongoing situation. We can label the subsequent crowdsourcing wave as a "Please share" process, where users of the social media spread the information not on their own initiative but at the request of the author, previous users who had shared the content, and the content itself. The content that was crowdsourced announced the start of humanitarian aid collections and first collection location. Having a crowd that was willing to share the humanitarian aid call consequently led to three support branches taken over by the crowd. First among these was related to the sharing of the content. People who shared the content (the humanitarian aid call) also brought humanitarian aid to the collecting point. At the same time, many others who had never shared the content through social media, but who were among social media users within the reach of crowdsourced sharing, decided to support the initiative by donating food or other necessary supplies. The second crowdsourcing branch was related to the collection logistics, which could be compared to the two levels of upside-down pyramids. Social media information spread triggered three additional collection initiatives at three different locations, but all of them were directly connected to the original informal response. The observed phenomenon relieved individuals, who began with the initiative, of additional effort to promote and distribute support calls or to organize collection of humanitarian aid. The crowd organized by itself in the following manner: one household gathered goods from neighbors and relatives and brought them to the collection point, where all the goods were stored until the transport collected them and delivered to the affected region. The third branch is similar to the humanitarian aid donation, but it is still specific by virtue of the fact that in the final part of the social media information chain were companies that contribute to the initiative by lending their own power generators. Individuals that participated in the power generators initiatives brought power devices with relatively low power capabilities, able to produce less than 1kW of power. Such generator can be used during short-term electricity loss in individual households; this is why 5kW and stronger generators owned by the companies that participated presented much higher contribution. The role of social media and the crowdsourced information spread was, in this case, to reach individuals who were able to influence decision-makers within the companies to lend the generators.

6 Social Media and Disaster Protection Standard Operating Procedures: Conceptual Optimization

Treating social media as an important communication channel is still far from being real. Even though the Administration for Civil Protection and Disaster Relief launched a crowdsourcing mobile application (Volba), its practical usage in emergency situations never contributed any valuable information due to the low number of users. After the consequences of the ice storm started to be revealed, the national flood standard operating procedure (SOP) was activated in order to proceed with the official response and deployment of regional civil protection teams and other services. The national SOP presents a closed frame within which is built regional and local response SOPs. Slight adjustments on local levels are generally acceptable, according to the characteristics of the local environment, while protruding innovations are banned from local level SOPs.

The conceptual optimization of a national flood SOP, presented in Figure 3, contributes to the official emergency response, and not merely in a way that was predicted for the Volba mobile application, which aimed to crowdsource information gathering from incident sites during natural disasters. It adds also information and alarm-raising capabilities that are not yet used to the fullest extent. We can divide the activities of the flood SOP workflow into four procedure types: collecting information, decision-making, responding, and sharing the information. Decision-making is directly connected to the information gathering that is implemented as site monitoring, and follows the online data of the Slovenian Environment Agency. Response activities are all actions taken on the field that are delegated to fire brigades, rescue responders and civil protection teams, according to previously made decisions and set response priorities. Sharing the information is a part of the alarm mechanism where regulations determine that after every alarm sign the explanation must be published. It can also be seen as part of the Administration for Civil Protection and Disaster Relief's obligation to publish public information, given that it is important for communities and individuals to be informed about the ongoing situation.

Social media response as an infrastructural element of the system that directly supports collecting and sharing information and indirectly allows decision-making and field response support improves the flood SOP without high additional effort. An important advantage of social media, social networking, information sharing, and online crowdsourcing workflow is that a small input can trigger an extensive response of the community that would otherwise stay out of the response activities. Activities of the SOP that in their core include collecting and sharing information present input for the social media response. Phase 1 remains under the control of the official responsible entity; it is part of the official response. During this phase, decisions are made as to what kind of support is needed from social media users and with what content to address them. Phase 2 evolves without possible efficient control or monitoring. During this phase users of social media respond according to their capabilities or motivation; in the case of information sharing by making that sharing viral, and in case of crowdsourcing by taking and sharing photos, videos or other data. Phase 3 is active only in cases of crowdsourcing through social media. It is an analytical phase where official entities gather and evaluate the crowdsourcing results and consequently decide whether to continue with the call or to stop it or whether there is a need to adjust the content of the call.

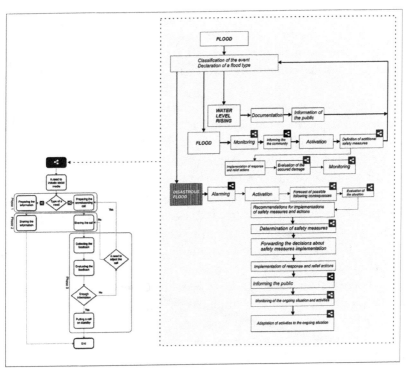

Fig. 3: Flood SOP – conceptual optimization

Even though it is hard to predict with certainty the precise social media response in further emergency situations similar to the ice storm, we have developed a general conceptual innovation based on the workflow frame. While we extracted the workflow from the analyzed ice storm case, this could be used in any other disaster situation, such as during floods in Bosnia, Serbia and Croatia in May 2014, where social media relayed crucial information about the coordination of field activities.

7 Discussion

Social media takes a very important role during the emergence of an informal response initiative that has been triggered by ongoing emergency events. It is a reliable communication channel, available even when conventional means of communication fail due to electric power failure, congestion or any other cause. Beside availability, a crucial feature of social media in emergencies is its accessibility, prevalence and, consequently, its global reach. Social media became a platform for communication, reconnaissance activities, decision-making support and, last but not least, crowdsourcing within the informal community that reacts and responds during emergency events.

Even though Slovenia maintains a formal disaster protection system that operates under a system of homeland security under the Administration for Civil Protection and Disaster Relief, the case study of the response after the ice storm clearly shows the importance of informal response initiatives based on the use of social media. The material damage and directly-following consequences created an extraordinary situation that cut affected households from the power, water and communication grid. Damaged road connections, deadly dangerous forest routes and a landscape covered with ice made it literally impossible for inhabitants of higher regions to meet the urban valley. The formal response of the entities included in the disaster response system was limited to the standard operating procedures and regulations of European Community mechanism for civil protection. It took actions based on response workflow diagrams for the disastrous situation of heavy flooding, because at the time of the ice storm there was no national, regional or local response standard that would define emergency activities after an ice storm.

Informal response activities began almost immediately after the ice storm. Social media took over information channel tasks, providing the citizens of the affected region with a platform on which to share first-hand information about the reality of the situation: the status of households, infrastructure, water and power supply immediately after the ice storm. Informal responders decided to get involved in the response process based on the information available through social media, notwithstanding that the time of their decision-making there was no available formal information saying that affected regions would need support other than that provided through official channels. Social media was further used as a platform for two important procedures within an informal response process. Initiatives used it as a crowdsourcing mechanism for collecting food, water and other necessary supplies, including power generators, that were transported to the local crisis response centers. In addition, initiatives used it for communication with responders and initiatives in the affected region and for the coordination of common activities.

From the presented process diagram, we clearly see what the temporal dynamic of the informal response was and how close it was connected to the capabilities of social media. According to the response process of the formal disaster protection system and the information provided by the Administration for Civil Protection and Disaster Relief, there would have been no need for any informal support: reality has shown them be wrong. From the graphic model that includes insights from this case study we can conclude that the Slovene disaster protection system lacks the efficient integration of social media and neglects the capabilities of the crowd and informal initiatives that are clearly able to use social media technology not just for everyday leisure time, but also as a very important platform for emergency response.

Acknowledgments

This research has been financed by the Slovenian Research Agency ARRS' Young Researcher Programme, ARRS-SP-2784/13. Creative Core FIS-NM-3330-13-500033 'Simulations' project funded by the European Union, the European Regional Development Fund. The operation is carried out within the framework of the Operational Programme for Strengthening

Regional Development Potentials for the period 2007–2013, Development Priority 1: Competitiveness and Research Excellence, Priority Guideline 1.1: Improving the Competitive Skills and Research Excellence.

References

Busch E Nathan / Givens D Austen: "Public-Private Partnerships in Homeland Security: Opportunities and Challenges." *Homeland Security Affairs*, 8(1), 2012.

Damij Talib: "An Object Oriented Methodology for Information Systems Development and Business Process Reengineering." *Journal of Object-Oriented Programming*, 13(4), 2000, pp. 23–34.

Frandsen Sanne / Morsing Mette / Vallentin Steen: "Adopting sustainability in the organization." *Journal of Management Development*, 32(3), 2013, pp. 236–246.

Gilfoil M DAvid: "Mapping Social Media Tools for Sell vs Buy Activities into Emerging and Developed Markets." *International Journal of Management & Information Systems*, 16(1), 2012, pp. 69–82.

Glassman R Bernardo: "Persistence and Loose Coupling in Living Systems." *Behavioral Science*, 18(2), 1973, pp. 83–99.

Grossberndt Sonja: "Application of Social Media in the Environment and Health Professional Community." *Environmental Health*, 11(1), 2012.

Holguín-Veras Jose / Taniguchi, Eiichi / Ferreira Filipa / Jaller Miguel / Thompson G Richard: "The Tohoku Disasters: Preliminary Findings Concerning the Post Disaster Humanitarian Logistics Response." 2012 Annual Meeting of the Transportation Research Board.

Koven G. Steven: "Image Construction in the Wake of Hurricane Katrina." *Public Organization Review*, 10(1), 2010, pp. 339–355.

Moilanen Sinikka: "Learning and the Loosely Coupled Elements of Control." *Journal of Accounting & Organizational Change*, 8(2), 2010, pp. 136–159.

O`Brien Geoff / O`Keefe Phil / Gadema Zaina / Swords Jon: "Approaching Disaster Management through Social Learning." *Disaster Prevention and Management*, 19(4), 2010, pp. 498–508.

Orton J D / Weick K E: "Loosely Coupled Systems: A Reconceptualization." *The Academy of Managerial Review*, 15(2), 1990, pp. 203–223.

Simula Henri / Töllinen Aarne / Karjaluoto Heikki: "Crowdsourcing in the Social Media Era: A Case Study of Industrial Marketers." *Journal of Marketing Development and Competitiveness*, 7(2), 2013, pp. 122–137.

URSZR: SPIN, Emergency Response Information System. Available via spin.sos112.si. http://spin.sos112.si/SPIN2/Javno/Porocila/ Accessed 29 May 2014.

Weick K. Edward: "Educational Organizations as Loosely Coupled Systems." *Administrative Science Quarterly*, 21(1), 1976, pp. 1–19.

Woerndl Maria / Papagiannidis Sawas / Bourlakis Michael / Li Feng: "Internet-induced Marketing Techniques: Critical Factors in Viral Marketing Campaigns." *International Journal of Business Science & Applied Management*, 3(1), 2008, pp. 33–45.

Xia Zhen / Liu Ji: "A Computational Approach to Characterizing the Impact of Social Influence on Individuals' Vaccination Decision Making." *PLoS One*, 8(4), 2013, pp. 1–11.

Željko Dobrović, Katarina Tomičić-Pupek
and Martina Tomičić Furjan
Faculty of Organization and Informatics, University of Zagreb

The Connection between a Process Model and a Data Model: A Metamodelling Approach

Abstract: Process modelling and data modelling appeared as methods in information systems development methodology. However, nowadays they are used as organisational methods in business process redesign efforts and documentation analysis and optimisation. These two methods are not completely independent. On the contrary, there is a strong natural relationship between them. Regardless of the way a process model was developed (data flow diagram, work flow diagram) it represents the starting point in data model development. All data flows (information flows) that appear in a process model contribute to the unique data model cumulatively, as their information content has been modelled. Therefore CASE tools that support process modelling and data modelling have some concepts in common. In this paper we explored these by using metamodelling.

Keywords: Process model, data model, metamodel

1 Introduction

Business process modelling and business data modelling are usually accepted as two activities in a range of activities in information systems development (ISD). For example, in accordance with information engineering methodology (Martin 1990), process modelling as a structural analysis of the system is a part of the main project of logical design of information systems (ISs), while data modelling is a part of the executional project of logical IS design.

The significance of process modelling and data modelling also lies in the construction of business and information architecture (Dobrović 2000, Cook 1996). There are three significant architectures: business, information, and technological. Business architecture represents the organisation structure, from top management to final operational levels, and is expressed in the form of a diagram with a description of jobs for each unit in the organisation. Top management runs the organisation supervising the implementation of the strategic plan in all business subsystems. The strategic planning of the information system results in information subsystems (Martin & Leben 1989). In most cases they do not correspond to the business subsystems, but they make a base for information management. Along with the process and data modelling for each information subsystem, information system strategic planning results in information architecture (Zachman 1987).

Business architectures contribute to clarify the complexity within an organisation and form a useful starting point from which to develop subsequent functional, information, process, and application architectures (Versteeg & Bouwman 2006).

Enterprise Architecting (EA) is the process of developing enterprise Information Technology architecture. An EA focuses on a holistic and integrated view of why, where, and who uses IT systems and how and what they are used for within an organisation. An enterprise architect develops the strategy and enables the decisions for designing, developing, and deploying IT systems to support the business as well as to assess, select, and integrate the technology into the organisation's infrastructure. Alignment between business and IT is one of the top issues for CIOs and IS managers (Armour, Kaisler, & Huizinga 2012).

Authors van Steenbergen and Brinkkemper introduce an architecture effectiveness model (AEM) to express how enterprise architecture practices are meant to contribute to the business goals of an organisation (van Steenbergen & Brinkkemper 2010). This paper introduces a Componentized Industry Business Architecture as a vehicle to address this gap and to make processes better integrated with other critical dimensions in organisational design. This architecture provides the foundation for a taxonomy of processes and enables process models to be created or potentially rationalized against a comprehensive framework (Sanz et al. 2012).

The main concepts describing information architecture are business process and information flow. Both form significant parts of the process model. Whichever process modelling method you use (Data Flow Diagram, Work Flow Diagram (Martin 1990), IDEF0 (Marca & McGowan 1993, U.S. NIST 1993) business processes will be modelled in each of them, and the obtained model will contain information flows (data flows). These information flows shall, after making the process model, be modelled individually, making up a unique data model of the organisation.

2 Process Modelling

The term "process", or the term "business process", which is used more and more nowadays, does not have a unique definition. The manner in which we view business process today has developed by transit of civilisation from the industrial into the information age in mid 1980s. The first definitions of the term process can be found in early 1970s. For example, in Buffa (1971) the term process usually means a manufacturing process. Back then, the most commonly used term was "operation/activity". The same book defines the framework of the manufacturing processes, and it is believed that such a term covered the entire range of activities performed fully manually, through semi-automatic systems, man–machine, to completely automatised processes, where a man as workforce has supervisory function only. The main characteristic of the process is transformation of input into output.

The administrative processes were clearly determined as processes transforming information. Their significance has begun to grow rapidly even then, since in the beginning of the 1970s the number of administrative workers in the USA surpassed the number of workers employed in the manufacturing department (Buffa 1971). It was then that the administrative processes started gaining significance and the term "integrated data processing system" first appeared. Business processes modelling was restricted to making assembly diagrams in the manufacturing processes, while there was no business processes modelling in the current IT sense of the word.

One of the first process modelling methods, SADT (Structured Analysis and Design Technique), was developed and tested "in the field" from 1969 to 1973 (Marca & McGowan 1993). Although that method enabled modelling of all types of processes, the term process in the original materials of this method is not used, but is replaced by term activity. In 1973, a form of this method was founded, called IDEF0 (Integrated DEFinition), which became a federal system (organisation) modelling standard in the USA and Europe (U.S. NIST 1993).

Even now, there is still no unique definition of a business process. Business process is described rather than defined. Therefore, in Havey (2005), a business process is described as "step-by-step rules specific for solution to a business problem". Apart from that, the process executes a range of activities in a certain time interval, in order to achieve a certain organisational goal. R. N. Khan (2004) defines a business process as a "range of activities performed in series or in parallel by two or more individuals or computer applications, in order to achieve the general goal of the organisation". According to the same author, business process modelling is a part of business process management, and business process management is the "area of modelling, automatizing, managing and optimizing business processes through their life cycle, in order to increase profitability".

Nowadays, processes are modelled with the help of different modelling methods. That is how we obtain different diagrams that describe business processes: data flow diagram (fig.1), work flow diagram (Mayer, Crump, & Fernandes 1995), IDEF0 diagram (Marca & McGowan 1993, U.S. NIST 1993).

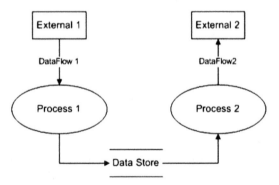

Fig. 1: Data Flow Diagram

2.1 Process Model Metamodel

In order to better understand the process model, and to facilitate the understanding of the connection between the process model and the data model, we define the process model metamodel. A metamodel is a "model about model" (Hay 2006) and it enables a CASE tool to be made, where the process modelling results would be kept for all organisations in which the processes were modelled.

To define the metamodel, it is necessary to understand the concepts of the process model. The process model, as a result of the logical design of the information system, answers this question: What is done in the organisation system? In order to make it as easy as possible to understand the answer to this question, a graphic representation of the process model is used in the form of e.g. a data flow diagram (DFD). A DFD (as shown in Figure 1) is a part of the structural system analysis method (SSA) and it is drawn up for each level of functional decomposition of the object system. The process of the highest level of the system represents the function, the medium level is the process level, and the lowest functional decomposition level is the set of activities. Although the function, process, and activity differ in the level of detailed description of the object system, they are all synonyms and we shall call them processes. Each process represents transformation of input data flow into output data flow; therefore data flow arises as the next concept of DFD. That is an organised set of data (a document, or verbal order, etc.) entering or exiting the process. The object system does not exist on its own, but is a part of some meaningful environment for information exchange. The external system represents the DFD concept which is the source of input data flow into the observed object system, or is the destination of the data flows that the monitored system generates. In a realistic object system there is always a time period between generating data and using them, and therefore the term "data store" is introduced to describe this characteristic in DFD. A data store represents interruption of the data flow control and brings a time delay between data generation in a single process and using the same by another process.

The process model metamodel (Figure 2) is a data model about the process model concepts. In other words, the metamodel contains data on processes, data stores, external systems, and data flows from the DFD of all levels of functional decomposition of the object system. The process modelling method enables a drafting of the process model, and its metamodel enables the retention and documenting of knowledge collected by that method. Apart from that, this metamodel forms the basis for the CASE tool to be made, supporting the process modelling method.

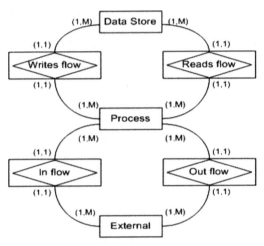

Fig.2: Basics of process model metamodel

To elaborate on Figure 2, the process, data store and external agents are three process model concepts that are independent, and therefore presented as separate entities. Data flow is a concept that is not independent, but represents the connection of other concepts; therefore it is displayed with four aggregations, depending on the concepts it connects. These aggregations are: *writes flow*, *reads flow*, *out_flow*, and *in_flow*. To be more precise, a process writes flow(s) into a data store, a process reads flow(s) from a data store, an external agent can give incoming flow(s) to a process, or an external agent can receive outgoing flow(s) from a process.

3 Data Modelling

Data modelling is an activity in the information system development that comes after the process modelling. We get the basis for business data modelling by collecting all information (data) flows between individual processes. The data modelling method (Bruce 1992) is a defined procedure of finding and displaying information objects (entities) and their mutual relationships (Figure 3).

The most commonly used model nowadays is relation data model, the basics of which are given in Chen (1976) and Codd (1970). The data model is often called the information model. That model is defined as "specification of data structures and business rules" (Bruce 1992). Data modelling is often called information modelling, and is defined as a "technique for describing information structures and preserving information on requirements and rules" (Bruce 1992).

3.1 Data Model Metamodel

One of the concepts that appears at DFD is the data flow (Figure 1). The process accepts the data flow as input, transforms it and generates a new data flow as its output. In case the organisation system is well-organised, all data flows appearing therein are standardised and formalised to a certain extent. Generally speaking, data flow is a set of data that are, in an ideal case, standardised throughout the relevant document. In an SSA method metamodel (Figure 2), data flows are kept in the following aggregations/ entities: *writes flow, reads flow, out_flow,* and *in_flow.*

The object of transformation executed by the business processes, from the point of view of the information system suitable for the same, is elementary data contained in one of the data flows recorded in the above aggregations, i.e. entities. However, it is not sufficient to list data flows (set of data) flowing into the system. All elementary data relevant to the functioning of the system, present in the data flows, must be presented as information objects that are interconnected in a certain way. The defined procedure of finding and displaying those information objects and their mutual relationship is called the data modelling method (Chen 1976).

The result of the application of the data modelling method is a data model (Figure 3). There are several data modelling methods. However, in this work the recommended method is the ER-entity relationship method and the accompanying entity relationship model.

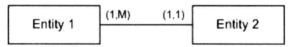

Fig. 3: Data model concepts

In order to give a clear, simplified, image of the data structure used by the organisation, we need to define the final set of concepts that we use to clarify information, objects, and the connections between them. The recommended entity relationship model metamodel has the basic concepts represented in Figure 4.

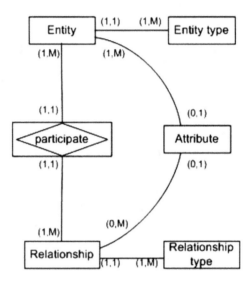

Fig. 4: Basics of the ER data model metamodel

The ENTITY concept represents the basic term of the entity relationship method (ER method) and marks an actual item or an abstract term that can be clearly distinguished from the environment. The ENTITY TYPE concept represents the different types of entities (weak, strong, aggregated). RELATIONSHIP is a concept marking a relationship existing between the entities, in reality or in thought. ATTRIBUTE is the name of the property a certain entity or relationship possesses. PARTICIPATE is an aggregated concept marking the participation of entities in different relationships. RE-LATIONSHIP TYPE is a concept that determines the type of relationship (identifying or non identifying).

The metamodel of the ER method is a data model on ER model concepts. This metamodel, as well as the process modelling method metamodel (Figure 2), has a double role: on one side it elaborates the ER method, clearly displaying relationships among the method concepts, and on the other side it represents the base for extending the data dictionary defined by the process model metamodel. Now we have basic elements to develop the integrated metamodel.

4 Connection between the Process Model and the Data Model – Common Integrated Metamodel

The connection between the business processes and business data is visible in the works of James Martin (Martin & Leben 1989, Martin 1990), where two sides of an information engineering pyramid are clearly shown: functional (process) and data. Apart from that, Zachman (1987) shows a process and data-based perspective of an organisation in its famous "information system architecture".

The natural way to show that the process model and data model are connected is through the common integrated metamodel of these two modelling methods. In other words, the results that we obtain through DFD and ER methods are in a way connected. Metamodels from Figures 2 and 4 will serve for that purpose. The manner of connecting them is defined in Figure 5.

The figure shows three sets of concepts (entities/aggregations). The left set contains the concept ENTITY, belonging to the ER method metamodel. On the other side, the right set contains aggregations which are the elements of the process modelling method metamodel, and they represent different forms of data flow of the organisational system. The set in the middle consists of aggregations containing the data flow modelling results of the system. In other words, middle concepts (WF STRUCTURE, RF STRUCTURE, IF STRUCTURE, OF STRUCTURE) represent the data structure of organisational data flows. For example, the WF STRUCTURE consists of all the entities that appeared while analysing data flows from the processes to data stores (Figure 2). In the same manner the RF STRUCTURE consists of all the entities that appeared while analysing data flows from data stores to processes. IF STRUCTURE and OF STRUCTURE relate to data flows from externals to processes, and from processes to externals, respectively.

The middle concepts in Figure 5 represent the intersection between the process model metamodel and the data model metamodel and serve as a basis for the development of an integrated repository of the CASE tool supporting process modelling and data modelling.

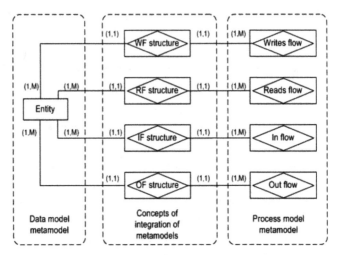

Fig. 5: Integration of process metamodel and data metamodel

5 Conclusion

The process model and data model are naturally connected, and the connection becomes obvious at the moment when we use the information system design methodology correctly. The process model responds to the question "What happens in the organisation?" The answer to that question is in the relevant process model, which occurs as a result of structural analysis of the system. Although the structural analysis of the system is a part of structural methods, it is well-known that the process model (function model) may be obtained by applying object analysis. In any case, the significant concepts of the process model are the process and data flow that connect the processes.

By taking over the data flows from the process model, and by modelling data in every data flow, we obtain a gradual wholesome data model of the organisation. The business data model obtained is translated into a relational form, in order to be able to use the same simply and efficiently in implementation of the relevant database in the selected database management system.

The process model and data model are connected by the concept of data flow from the process model. This connection is the most visible if we observe the process model and the data model through the relevant integrated metamodel, the basics of which are proposed in this paper. A metamodel has dual purpose: (1) it enables understanding of the very procedure of process and data modelling, and (2) it represents the basis for drawing up the CASE tool for supporting the information system of the organisation.

References

Armour, Frank / Kaisler, Steve / Huizinga, Edwin: "Introduction to Business and Enterprise Architecture: Processes, Approaches and Challenges Minitrack." *System Science (HICSS), 45th Hawaii International Conference* (3), 2012, pp. 24–29.

Bruce, Thomas A.: *Designing Quality Databases with IDEF1x Information Models*. Dorset House, USA, 1992.

Buffa, Elwood S.: *Basic Production Management*. J. Wiley & Sons, USA, 1971.

Chen Peter P. S.: "The Entity-Relationship Model – Toward a Unified View of Data." *ACM Transactions on Database Systems* 1(1), 1976, pp. 9–36.

Codd Edgar F.: "A Relationship Model of Data for Large Shared Databases." *Communications of the ACM* 13(6), 1970, pp. 377–387.

Cook Melissa A.: *Building Enterprise Information Architectures*. Prentice Hall, USA, 1996.

Dobrović, Željko: "Strategijsko Planiranje, Poslovna i Informacijska Arhitektura." *Proceedings of CASE 12 Conference*, 2000, pp. 60–72.

Havey, Michael: *Essential Business Process Modelling*. O'Reilly Media Inc., CA, 2005.

Hay, David C.: *Data Model Patterns – A Metadata Map*. Morgan Kaufmann Publishers, USA, 2006.

Khan, Rashid N.: *Business Process Management*. Meghan-Kiffer Press, USA, 2004.

Marca, David A. / McGowan, Clarence L.: *IDEF0/SADT – Business Process and Enterprise Modelling*. Eclectic Solutions, CA, 1993.

Martin, James: *Information Engineering, I, II, III*. Prentice Hall, Englewood Cliffs, New Jersey, 1990.

Martin, James / Leben, Joe: *Strategic Information Planning Methodologies*. Prentice-Hall, USA, 1989.

Mayer, Richard J. / Crump, John W. / Fernandes, Ronald: *IDEF Methods – Compendium of Methods Report*. Armstrong Laboratory, Wright-Patterson, Ohio, 1995.

Sanz, Jorge L. C. / Leung, Ying / Terrizzano, Ignacio / Becker, Valeria / Glissmann, Suzanne / Kramer, Joseph / Ren, Guang-Jie: "Industry Operations Architecture for Business Process Model Collections." *Business Process Management Workshops, Lecture Notes in Business Information Processing* (100), 2012, pp. 62–74.

van Steenbergen, Marlies / Brinkkemper, Sjaak: "Modeling the Contribution of Enterprise Architecture Practice to the Achievement of Business Goals." *Information Systems Development 2010*, 2010, pp. 609–618.

U.S. NIST (National Institute of Standards and Technology), DISA (Defence Information Systems Agency): *Integration Definition for Function Modeling (IDEF0), Federal Information Processing Standards*, Publication 183, 1993.

Versteeg, Gerrit / Bouwman, Harry: "Business Architecture: A New Paradigm to Relate Business Strategy to ICT". *Information Systems Frontiers* 8(2), 2006, pp. 91–102.

Zachman, John A.: "A Framework for Information Systems Architecture." *IBM Systems Journal* 26(3), 1987, pp. 276–292.

Jernej Agrež and Nadja Damij
Faculty of Information Studies in Novo mesto, Slovenia

Business Process Management: Evolution Blueprint and Practical Implementation

Abstract: The purpose of this paper is to explore business process management evolution, determine the state of existing knowledge and apply a business process management methodology to a test case. We conducted a literature review to determine characteristics of the development of business process management over time. Among the addressed methodologies, we selected the most appropriate for process simulation and compared their modeling and simulation capabilities. Our comparison led us to select the Tabular application development methodology, used to build a missing person incident investigation process model that we further translated into the process simulation within the iGrafx simulation environment. The contribution of this paper consists of the business process management evolution blueprint, and its novel approach to the assessment of the public safety incident from the process management perspective.

Keywords: Business process management, process modeling, process improvement, process simulation

1 Introduction

Taking into consideration a commonly used set of approaches for organizational optimization, it cannot be denied that the foundations of process management have been recognized as important tool of modern organizations. Defining a process as a primary focus is enabling organizations to create a new base for establishing flexible, productive and innovative organizational environment. The process management chains together increase organizational optimization and product quality value, but in addition to this they also give us a wide, and at the same time precise, perspective into observing, analyzing and manipulating organizational behavior.

Process management has been present in the field of public safety for a long time in the form of standard procedures and regulations that define how field and administration work have to be carried out. Although public safety services base their actions on predefined processes, they face events that on a daily basis present risky and highly unstable environments where changes occur in unpredicted and uncontrolled manners. One of such example is that of the missing person incident (MPI), which is a very fragile part of the field of public safety. It is of great importance that we can assess and analyze this field in a virtual environment, but with a scenario based on real life.

In the first part of this paper we present the theoretical background of process management, together with its conceptual evolution from its early beginnings to predictions of future trends. We continue by selection, detailed description and comparison of process modeling approaches that allow translation of the model into the process based simulation, and thereafter use a selected process modeling method to analyze the MPI and translate it into the simulation, where we separated activity flow from decision-making to be able to observe the behavior of every single entity, and the influences and dependencies that they create.

The findings of the research propose an analytical modeling and simulation solution that can be used for complex processes such as MPI cases. Although we used a single case for setting up the modeling and simulation structure, we designed it in a flexible manner so as to be able to insert new or discard existing entities as well as calibrate their behavior patterns, according to data collected from new MPI cases.

2 Method

For the first part of the research we reviewed the existing literature, studying cases and relevant research that directly included process management or held a connection with the concept. With the gathered information we constructed a conceptual graphical model of the evolution of process management from its early beginnings until today. We then selected business process modeling techniques and undertook a tabular comparison, so as to be able to select a method for the third, practical, part of our research. In this part we firstly used the observation method for collecting the data that we needed to create a process diagram of our case study. Through this, we were able to define the process-based behavior of 14 different institutions, organizations, informal groups and individuals who took a direct role within the case study. We carefully recorded 88 different activities within the process and entity-based patterns that took the place during the process. Data for the study was gathered in May 2013 and thereafter processed with a TAD methodology that was selected by previously comparing different business process management analytical approaches. For the purpose of the process simulation and analysis we used an iGrafx process simulation environment that allowed us to separate the main activity flow from decision-making, but at the same time make them interdependent.

3 Process Management's Theoretical Background

Process management chains together the organizational optimization and product quality value: "if one takes care of the process, the product will take care of itself; and any result is part of an endless process leading to future results and future processes" (Chung 2009, p. 187). Once we develop or apply a process model to a business system, it will "help to produce more timely and accurate information leading to better decision making, help to improve transparency leading to better risk management, and help to improve auditing operations leading to lower compliance costs" (Cernaushas & Tartantino 2009, p. 16). Different process-oriented approaches are set up on the same basic elements of business process recognition, description and modification that provide the framework for necessary adjustments or improvements within the organizational environment. "However, it is very dangerous to assume that simply copying either the business processes or the approach towards their improvement from one successful case to another will bring the same benefits" (Trkman 2010, p. 127). This is why, while defining optimization solutions, a variety of options are available including applying the open sets with already defined and specific process-oriented models measuring a development of innovative solutions for localized issues, which include "gathering the information related to processes from different sources, monitoring these processes, and aligning them with corporate strategies and high-level goals" (Pourshahid et al. 2009, p. 271).

To improve labor productivity, Frederick Winslow Taylor was, in the 19th century, the first known person to study different aspects of workers' characteristics. His management model was set on the "practical specialization of work activities" (Taylor 1911, p. 14). In this time parallel we cannot neglect Henry Fayol. Brunson found his argument about management being close to the majority of organizations to be a durable idea (Brunson 2008). At the same time, Gantt designed a tool later named the Gantt chart that could be marked as the "very first process model ever used" (Gantt, 1913). Taylor's work was followed and upgraded by Henry Ford who developed "a concept that was based on the principles of product standardization, use of specialized equipment and reduction of workers` specialization for purpose of production" (Tolliday & Zeitlin 1987, p. 6) and by Frank Bunker Gilbreth Sr. who introduced Therbligs – "elemental work motions with the aim to improve work results through the constant improvement of the working conditions (Nanda 2006, p. 188). According to George (1968, p. 207) he was the first person to introduce the Flowchart and Functional Flow Block Diagram (FFBD) and according to Reeves (1994, p. 419) the first who implemented the basic cyclic approach, an introduction in total quality management. The 1960s brought the Petri net process modeling technique, which became popular in "modeling and analyzing different kind of processes, from protocols to business processes" (van der Aalst 1998, p. 23). In the 1970s "IDEF0 was developed, by the US military for conducting analysis and estimations, and later evolved in its higher versions" (Grover & Kettinger 2000, p. 168). Post-Fordism brought fundamental changes, compared to Ford's philosophy: "the production line work got replaced by an approach that supported learning, motivation and provision of know-how, to be able to guarantee the dynamic answers to the market demands" (McDowell 1991, p. 400).

In the early 1980s we can also find the first mention of a theory of constraints, which "brought new ideas about business planning that attracted many executives and production planners" (Rand 2000, p. 173), as well as "total quality management" (Powell 1995, p. 15). In this decade the "Toyota production system directed Toyota Company on [its] way towards one of the largest auto producers in the world" (Fujimoto 1999, p. 3) and, a few years later, Porter (1985, p. 36) labeled 1985 a year of the "value chain" as a new presentation of organizations' activities. The 1990s began with the Rummler-Brache methodology, described in their book *Improving Performance* together with the business process improvement (also known as business process redesign), described in James Harrington's *Business Process Improvement: The Breakthrough Strategy for Total Quality, Productivity, and Competitiveness* (1991). This is the period of business process reengineering (also known as business process innovation), which is defined as the "global innovation and thorough change of business processes to achieve important improvements in performance measures such as cost, quality, service and speed of production" (Hammer 1993, p. 2), wherein "enterprise resource planning was deployed and promoted among executives officers" (Umble 2003, p. 251) and "lean production, derived from TPS and influenced by Taylorism and Fordism, began its successful march" (Womack & Jones 2003, p. 7). Gupta (2009, p. 3) spread the importance of a process-based link with knowledge, today known as learning organization, together with Nonaka, who advocated understanding knowledge within the frames of knowledge management. A "capability maturity model was developed that included set of criteria that can serve to improve organizational development processes" (Paulk 1993, p. 30). Benchmarking was for the first time described as a business tool in Boxwell's (1994, p. 157) Benchmarking for Competitive Advantage, and, soon after, there was "notable six sigma breakthrough in General Electric" (Eckes 2001, p. 1) together with "workflow management and its main purpose systematic process oriented approach" (van der Aalst 1998, p. 25). In the 21st century there has been expanded "supply chain management, connecting organizations that ran operational and managerial value-adding processes" (Lampert & Cooper 2000, p. 70). According to Hüffner (2004, p. 25) capability maturity model further evolved in the business process maturity model, while "process architecture based management got introduced through service oriented architecture which revealed component based process view" (Bieberstein 2008, p. 1), and process automation appeared together with enterprise application integration. "Both are symbiotically incorporated in process modeling" (Linthicum 2003, p. 2), and "business process collaboration became a very important part of modern global business development" (Gong et al. 2006, p. 14). Business process mining appeared as a useful tool for process identification and definition, "extracting knowledge about processes from their transactional log files" (van der Aalst et al. 2002, p. 21). In 2011, Business Process Model and Notation 2.0 was released, and replaced the first generation of BPMN and became a "standardized notation for writing down the business processes" (Allwayer 2010, p. 2). With the rapid development of IT technology, influences can be seen also at IS and its business part is not excluded. "Real-time business intelligence is becoming decision driver, disabling process slowdown, and supporting transformation from short term process management" (Plenkiewicz 2010, p. 59) in "day to day process management" (Cohen 2010, p. 1), and, finally, in "real-time process management" (Smith & Fingar 2002, p. 5). It is not hard to indicate that from its early scientific beginnings until today the development of the following vertical structure can be distinguished: first, process modeling and, second, process improvement. Each of these contains many different approaches that use a specific set of methods. From the horizontal point of view, such a structure is intertwined with similar western or eastern influences that are necessary for establishing connections and enabling synergies among approaches and methodologies. Such synergies produced market products, suites that became known as business process management systems (BPMS) that contain different solutions for specific demands and allow tailored accession to optimal results. BPMS can be identified as the latest generation in the process management concept because, after a century of the development, testing and spreading of process management structures, modern systems are trying to merge together to get the best use out of it: the perfect elements that will provide the demanded solutions.

4 Process Management's Conceptual Evolution

In the early beginning of the research we discovered uncertainty among basic definitions concerning process management or business process management. "Process management, based on a view of an organization as a system of interlinked processes, involves concerted efforts to map, improve, and adhere to organizational processes" (Benner & Tushman 2001, p. 241). We define business process management as follows: "Supporting business processes using methods, techniques, and software to design, enact, control, and analyze operational processes involving humans, organizations, applications, documents and other sources of information" (van der Aalst, Hofstede & Weske 2003, p. 4). In trying to understand the difference between two definitions we must define the difference between the processes that are their primal focus. A process is a completely closed, timely and logical sequence of activities, which is required to work on a process-oriented business object. Such process-oriented object can be, for example, "an invoice, a purchase order or a specimen" (Becker, Kugeler &

Rosseman 2003, p. 2). A business process is simply how an organization does its work – "the set of activities it pursues to accomplish a particular objective for a particular customer, either internal or external" (Davenport 2005, p. 4). The conceptual evolution map (Figure 1) enables us to get a clearer picture of process management's historical changes. The first half of our proposed timeline presents approaches such as Taylorism, Fayolism, Fordism and quality control that are representatives of constructed approaches, using several perspectives to achieve process development and optimization. On the other hand we can recognize approaches such as Gantt charts, Flowcharts, Functional Flow Block Diagram, Petri net and Therbligs which are used mostly for process description and explanation, without integrated tools to directly increase the process optimization level. The following two decades defined, on one hand, strong approaches, such as the theory of constraints, the Toyota production system and total quality management, that provided the ability to change and improve addressed processes, while, on the other, provided new IDEF modeling approaches such as IDEF0, IDEF1, IDEF1X and IDEF3.

Searching for connections among modeling approaches from 1900 until 1980, we notice the following similarities. In the first stage, the Gantt chart acts as predecessor of the Flowchart and Functional Flow Block Diagram which can be also further evolved into the Flowchart with elements of Therblings (additional elements with new meanings). Fordism acted as an influence on later Taylorism. In the second stage, the Flowchart and Functional Flow Block Diagram present a clear foundation for the development of Petri net and IDEF0 which use similar graphic notation for the presentation of connections and activities. At the end of the period IDEF0 evolved in versions 1–3, which use very similar notation for information modeling, data modeling and process modeling. The improvement approaches in this stage represent the connection between quality control and total quality management. Less clear but notable is the connection between these quality twins and the Toyota production system. The latter was originally called "just-in-time production" and evolved into a modern general just-in-time philosophy that includes some elements of quality-oriented approaches. The theory of constraints uses different, constraint-elimination focused logic that highlights no obvious connection with the others in this period. Post-Fordism appeared as an answer to the market demands and implemented a contra-Fordism approach. Some similarities with Taylorism could be found. In the period after 1980, during the third stage, there was a notable expansion of different approaches associated with improvement as well as modeling. The IDEF pool got versions 4 (object-oriented design) and 5 (ontology description capture) and benchmarking was introduced as a qualitative modeling approach. We can see connections between the capability maturity model and business process maturity which addresses CMM's process-oriented features. There is also an evolving connection between Petri nets and Workflow management. In this stage BPMN became standard in process modeling and in a short time evolved from first to second generation. Service-oriented architecture, complex and not primarily used for business process modeling, can be, when graphically presented, compared with earlier approaches like Petri net or IDEF pool. The business process mining philosophy that stands on the timeline in front of all modeling approaches derived out of data mining to enable process modeling in an environment where other approaches fail to produce satisfactory results. In the third stage of the process improvement, evolution links get harder to distinguish, because of the new emerging interactions among process improvement techniques.

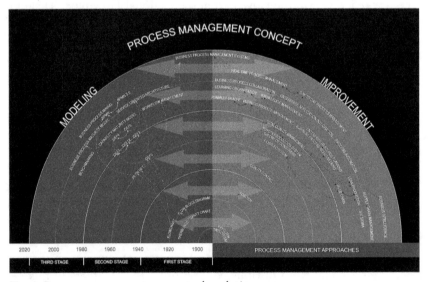

Fig. 1: Process management conceptual evolution map

i. knowledge (learning organization in interaction with knowledge man-
    agement) influenced by the Toyota production system;
ii. process core change (business process improvement in interaction
    with Rummler-Brache, business process reengineering) influenced by
    post-Fordism;
iii. IT based (enterprise resource planning, enterprise application integra-
    tion, process automation, business process collaboration) influenced by
    the Toyota production system;
iv. interdisciplinary (business intelligence, supply chain management, six
    sigma) influenced by total quality management;
v. quality (value chain and its successor, lean production) influenced by the
    Toyota production system, total quality management and post-Fordism;
vi. constraints (day to day process management in interaction with re-
    al-time process management), influenced by the theory of constraints
    and the Toyota production system.

5 Process Modeling for Further Simulation

Greasley (2003, p. 420) finds process simulation to be a useful tool in
change management within business systems. Kano et al. (2005, p. 690)
argue it holds powerful analytical capability for evaluating business solutions, while Maruster and van Beest (2009, p. 271), in their case study,
apply simulation dynamics to workflow models of activities and transactions among them. Approaches to business process simulation are set
on comparable logics and used for similar purposes, and even though we
cannot neglect discrepancies in details of individual modeling techniques,
this serves as a starting platform for simulation development. Not every
modeling technique is appropriate for simulation of any process dynamic,
especially when our aim is to simulate process characteristics that were
originally not meant as primary source of simulation.

For purpose of this research we will set our research problem scope to
determine which of selected process modeling techniques shows the highest
predisposition to being used for purposes of the development and testing
of external scenarios and integration into the originally estimated business
process simulation framework. We want to define a usable, simple to understand and near intuitive simulation environment that will be "layer-based"

(Chen et al. 2013, p. 2068) and "grid oriented" (Yin 2010, p. 276) and will allow us theoretical simulation, applicable to practical problems, concerned with integration of business process management and activity flow scenario analyses.

Process modeling with IDEF0 rules is a method based on a function which is defined as "a set of activities that takes certain inputs and by means of some mechanism, and subject to certain control, transforms the inputs into outputs" (Kim & Kim 2007, p. 6). It uses the ICOM (Input, Control, Output, and Mechanism) concept as a main process presentation. "Function transforms inputs into outputs under the influence of a control, using the mechanisms provided. Inputs and outputs are information or physical objects. Controls activate or regulate or synchronize the function. Mechanisms are resources necessary to perform function. ICOM boxes are connected by arrows; outputs of one box can be inputs or controls of other boxes" (Kacprzak & Kaczmarczyk 2006, p. 591). "IDEF0 modeling is simple and its notation is standard enough that it can be easily transformed in normalized database what practice results in many applications, developed on such" (Hastings & Funk 2008, p. 1177).

On the other hand time, such a modeling approach causes an inability to note the time dimension, or to define correctness or conformity criteria in the model itself. The "possibility exists to detect and highlight model incorrectness when it is originating in failure to follow the schematic modeling rules" (Kacprzak & Kaczmarczyk 2006, p. 589).

We use IDEF3 for a description of process flow. Plaila and Carrie (1995, p. 3) described it as modeling method that enables us to discern what the estimated system optimization is and to predict the new process model. It presents "the behavioral aspects of an existing or proposed system" (IDEF 2013). The most significant difference between IDEF0 and IDEF3 is that "IDEF3 does not let us create a model of the system, but captures precedence and causality relations between situation and events in a form that is natural to domain experts" (Plaila & Carrie 1995, p. 3). Models contain four types of elements as described by Kim, Yim and Weston (2001, p. 320) as units of behavior (they define objects, time intervals in which they occur, and relationships with other processes), junctions (logical mechanisms that define the time and relationship of a single unit of behavior), links (they define the destination of a single unit of behavior) and referents (additional information about a single unit of behavior).

"TAD (tabular application development) is an object-oriented methodology. This methodology describes the functioning of the organization using several tables" (Damij 2000, p. 24). According to Damij (2007, p. 70), the TAD approach results in a tabular description and presentation of the business process environment. It consists of an entity table that defines and describes all subjects and their associations within the business system. The next table is named the activity table and maps every single activity that operates as a part of the process and, going even further, we have designed a task table that defines connection between entities and work tasks within every activity in the process.

"Each activity occupies one row of the table. A non-empty square (i, j) shows a certain task or work represented by the activity defined in row i performed by an entity defined in column j. Developing the activity table is a result of interviews organized with the internal entities defined in the columns of the table. In the rows of the activity table we first register each activity identified during an interview and then link this activity with the entities in the columns, which cooperate in carrying it out. To make the activity table represent the real world, we link the activities horizontally and vertically. The purpose of defining horizontal and vertical connections is to define their similarity to the real world in which they occur" (Damij 2000, p. 25).

"The classical Petri net is a directed bipartite graph with two node types called places and transitions. The nodes are connected via directed arcs. Connections between two nodes of the same type are not allowed. Places are represented by circles and transitions by rectangles. ...When every place incident on a transition is marked, that transition is said to be enabled. An enabled transition may fire by putting one token into each of its output places" (Han & Young 2012, p. 46). Bobbio (1990, p. 4) describes a Petri net as a graphical visualization of activity flow within a complex system. Further, comparing the approach with other similar modeling techniques, she finds Petri net an appropriate way to describe "logical interactions among parts or activities in a system. Typical situations that can be modelled by PN are synchronization, sequentiality, concurrency and conflict"

Bobbio (1990, p. 4); they have been "applied mostly in manufacturing and safety-critical systems" (Peleg et al. 2005, p .198).

"Gantt charts are widely used to represent production plans, schedules, and actual performance" (Jones 1988, p. 893). Pankaja (2005 p. 14) defines a Gantt chart as a graphical representation of the work breakdown structure, combined with total time duration defined for single task; entities delegated to the tasks and overall process completion percentage. "Gantt gave two principles for his charts: one, measure activities by the amount of time needed to complete them; two, use the space on the chart to represent the amount of the activity that should have been done in that time" (Herrmann 2010, p. 247). Wilson (2003, p. 437) further develops this definition, explaining that Gantt chart logic uses systemic solutions and pays no attention to the algorithmic solving of the problem. "In a Gantt chart, each task takes up one row. Dates run along the top in increments of days, weeks, or months, depending on the total length of the project. The expected time for each task is represented by a horizontal bar whose left end marks the beginning of the task and the right end marks the completion of task" (Pankaja 2005, p. 20).

BPMN is a modeling approach that consists of a graphical representation describing the business process on the control–flow base with core graphical elements and an extended specialized set. Recker et al. (2006, p. 335) define the core elements as a set that provides a graphical presentation for substantial business processes in simple, intuitive models, which together with an extended specialized set, enables the presentation of advanced problems, such as "orchestration and choreography, workflow specification, event-based decision making and exception handling" (Recker et al. 2006, p. 335). The approach is easy to understand and clear to interpret, but, as Lerner et al. (2010, p. 165) find out, not supported by formal semantic background. Lack of formalisation can cause a different interpretation of the similar process models. A similar deficiency is described by Recker et al. (2006, p. 339), who write about the lack of precisely defined and integrated common business rules, which cause an additional need that the user is forced to improve by himself.

Table 1: Modeling approaches comparison

No.	Modeling approach	Type of mapping and notation	Syntax components (process components)
1.	IDEF0	semantically supported graphical diagram	box (function), arrow (input, control, output, mechanism, call)
2.	IDEF3	semantically supported graphical diagram	process schematics: box (unit of behavior), arrows (links); object schematics: circle (object), label (object state), arrows (links)
3.	Tabular application development	symbol based notation	entity (letter & numeric symbol), activity (letter & numeric symbol)
4.	Petri net	bipartite directed graph, symbol based notation	circle (place), bar (transition), arc from place to transition (transition input relation), arc from transition to place (transition output relation), black dot (number of tokens)
5.	Gantt chart	semantically supported tabular/ graphical diagram	timeline (time window), tabular columns (task, task hierarchy, task duration)
6.	Business process model and notation	syntax modeling, graphical diagram	circle (activity), box (activity), diamond (gateway), full arrow (sequence flow), dashed arrow (message flow), dashed line (association)

Table 2: Modeling approaches comparison

No.	Primary dynamic	Secondary dynamic	Model hierarchy	Integration possibility
1.	function representing activity, process or transformation	fork (division), join (merger), node (parent box)	top-down decomposition	business process management, knowledge management, software engineering
2.	relations between situations and events	junctions (and, synchronous and, or, xor)	Situation/ event based order	business process management, software engineering

No.	Primary dynamic	Secondary dynamic	Model hierarchy	Integration possibility
3.	activity flow	decision (2 level division)	activity based order	business process management, knowledge management, software engineering
4.	token flow	complex logical interactions	transition based order	business process management, knowledge management, information system engineering, reliability engineering, diagnosis, simulations
5.	accomplishment of a task in time	task order hierarchy	time and accomplishment based order	project management
6.	events, activity flow	looping, nesting, process break, transactions, sub processing,	activity based order	organizational modeling, function modeling, data flow modeling

6 TAD, Practical Application and Process Simulation

"TAD represents simple concept for description of the organization using several tables" (Damij 2000, p. 23). Originally intended for information systems development and business process reengineering, it can be adopted for modeling a complex system. The first and second phases of TAD methodology include the framework, how to capture and map system functionality that include the entity table, activity table and task table. TAD methodology enables the creation of a model with any number of agent approximations (AA) that can incorporate any number of activities. We define AA as a decision-making individual, pair or group of people modeled on a basis of real-life events. Therefore such a model precisely summarizes process reality and maps it in the digital environment. On the other hand, the reality-based facts do not allow us to design true agents that would have the possibility of fully independent decision-making. Their actions are limited by activities and decisions that are part of modeled process.

The following real-life case is based on events that took place in May 2013. The entities involved in the MPI were: the victim, the victim's family, a police patrol, the police call center, an individual police officer, the human rights Ombudsman, the Prosecution service, the public, SAR responders and the distress-call center. Due to privacy concerns, no personal information that could reveal the identity of those who were involved in the case will be revealed. The time scope of the incident was defined to be seven days most important activities that took place within this timeframe. Even though the roots of the incident reach far back in the past, and the consequences could be present for a long time in the future, we will not include them in the scope of our research due to their indirect connection with the topic we present. Those MIP activities that remain in our research scope can be divided into days.

Day 1: the victim cleared internet history, temporary internet files, cookies and trash bin contents with Ccleaner – a software tool for PC optimization and cleaning.

Day 2: the victim left home between 8am and 3pm. Victim was seen in public twice on this day. The first contact was 0,5 kilometers away from home and the second contact was around 4pm and 1,8 kilometer away from home, heading in approximately a NNW direction.

Day 3: the victim was identified on a cash machine surveillance camera recording approximately 40 kilometers away from home. There was a new direction to the victim's movements, NW.

Day 4: the victim's family asks for SAR responders to support the search.

Day 5: the victim was seen 66 kilometers away from home. Heading remains the same – NW. The victim's family made contact with the human rights Ombudsman and the Prosecution Service due to their dissatisfaction with the police work. At around 10pm the family received an e-mail from the victim, explaining that the victim was alive and expressing a few thoughts about dissatisfaction in life.

Day 6: The victim was found by family approximately 80 kilometers away from home in a shelter for homeless people.

Day 7: The victim made contact with SAR responders and eventually they met, discussed the situation and decided how to close the case in constructive way.

We began the model with identification of the entities that will take the role of agent approximations. We adopted the TAD methodology's entity table and "adjusted it in the form of a matric system" (Agrež & Damij 2013, p. 172), to be able to present how each AA influences another. At this point we defined the following AA roles: influencing AA (the one that triggers influence), influenced AA (the one that changes behavior under influence) and neutral AA (the one who influences only activity flow). Furthermore, we mapped MPI activity flow with the TAD activity table, excluding any decision-making. The activity flow consists of one beginning and one end, and in between all activities are lined up within the time order as it was in the real situation. As the activity flow had already taken the place in the past, any additional decision-making would present deviation from captured reality. From the perspective of the present, the activity flow is predetermined and should not be treated differently. Adjustments to the activity table were as follows: We added a column that defined the time dimension of the process and at the same time we implemented coloring of the patterns, due to the weakly defined business process–work process relations of the MPI. Coloring of the patterns together with tabular separation reveals work processes within weakly defined environment more clearly and makes it easier to understand the process intuitively. Furthermore we added the agent approximation matrix and model decision-making agent approximations in additional layers of the activity table. Agent approximations were based on the decision-making that follows predefined protocols, law-based directives, past experiences and knowledge, personal judgment, prejudice, emotional liability, or any other kind of influence. Not every agent approximation consists of all possible influences, but it is important to not neglect those that could importantly deviate their modeled behavior. We adjusted the activity table in a way that one agent approximation replaced several organizational departments and different kinds of influences replaced the entities. If we had previously defined interaction in the agent approximation matrix, we must now include AA as influence as well, but at the same time we must define such relation as an activity influencing the AA, otherwise the influence is never realized but exists only as possibility. With the activity layer and AA layers we had already a general insight into influences in directions: influencing AA–influenced AA and influencing/influenced/neutral AA–activity flow. If the decision-making of a single AA would be elemental, hierarchical and would not interfere within itself, the number of possible AA influences would evolve in a predictable manner. Such a process would be simple to analyze but in fact it is far from real-life public safety processes. As a result of the high complexity of AA influences, it is necessary for us to develop a simulation that will incorporate and connect activity flow together with AA influences. For this purpose we translated the activity flow and AA tables into iGrafx process diagrams, as shown in Figure 2.

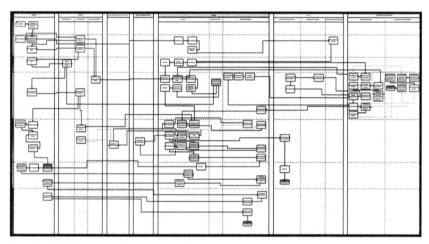

Fig. 2: MPI investigation process diagram

To be able to include every AA into the activity flow as an influence, we designed the whole MPI in single process layer, but created different starting points for each specific AA and for the activity flow. This is necessary for the AA to run with an independent trigger that send an activation signal (transaction). Furthermore we created the influence connection points, previously identified with TAD. For this purpose we used the attributes that are similar to the programming variables and can communicate data (information) and manage the flow of transactions through a process. For example, the attributes can set the duration of an activity based on the specifics of a transaction, control the flow of specific transactions through a decision output, or set global controls that can affect multiple transactions or activities. Through AA influences that are simulated as yes/no or true/false decisions and through the activity attributes we designed process scenario that reflected the real MPI investigation. To be able to analyze it we ran the simulation with predefined analytical queries based on transaction count within the activity flow and decision-making within every single AA supported by the statistically-based business process management approach six sigma.

7 Discussion

Levers of process management have been the subject of research by scientists, professionals and different organizations from the beginning of 20th century. With this paper we contribute to clearer identification of how the process management concept developed through the century from both a time and interaction perspective. As a starting point of the research, we took the earliest mentioning of management as a part of science and then we divided the 20th and beginning of 21st century into three separate periods of 40 years. In this time window, research indicates two general branches of process management concept evolution: the modeling branch which sets its scope among identification, definition and mapping, and the improvement branch that aims towards optimization. Within these two branches we can witness the appearance of different approaches among which some triggered further development of the whole branch or influenced long-term concept evolution. In the modeling branch we can observe how approaches from the first stage maintained their influence through the second stage until the third one, when they hit the expansion of approaches. The improvement branch shows us a notable foundation in the first stage which had lost its influence by the second half of the second stage, and which indicates a strong introduction in the third stage where expansion occurs in the same time parallel with modeling branch. Even though we addressed both branches individually we cannot neglect their constant interaction, which becomes even more apparent in the beginning of 21st century under the introduction of business process management systems.

When selecting the most appropriate process modeling method that will allow further integration into the simulation environment, we took in consideration following criteria: 1) definition of organizational system framework, 2) translation in process-based layers, 3) development and integration of scenario layers, and 4) integration of additional event layers. Among six compared modeling techniques we selected the TAD methodology which provided us with the most precise definition of an organizational system, the simplest, tabular-based multiple layer solution, and a highly flexible environment for the modeling and integration of any kind of scenarios and events. As a result of its range of abilities, we chose TAD as a predecessor to process simulation in the iGrafx environment.

A development of the proposed process simulation solution and MPI case application provided us with the important answers concerning activity flow and decision-making within the process. We were able to determine the high importance of the family's initiative to do whatever was necessary to find the missing person. As well as this, we detected the crucial interaction among community, family and private support which provided a wide range of special knowledge and information as well as the sustaining of momentum. Such tripartite interaction represents a critical element for the desired output of the process to be realized. The absence of any of these three elements would consequently lead to an alternative ending that can only be predicted as a what-if scenario and would not necessarily be realized. The simulation gave us another important insight to an MPI: partial endings of the process that are still treated as successful output even though the process itself never reaches the end as it had happened in the real case. Such partial endings are highly correlated with the family's priorities defining how far the family wants to go into the investigation process. At the same time, the results show us that if such partial ends exist, other entities involved in process could take the partial end as the final end, according to their regulations, practices, etc., and drop out of the activity flow. The work of entities that are considered public services presented 18 % of all activities within the investigation. The remaining 82 % of activities were conducted by two groups of entities; the major group with 64 % of activities represents the people that were involved in investigation in a completely private manner, and 18 % represents the entities that used their official public status to provide information and knowledge to the private investigation. In fact they were acting against the law and could be prosecuted for abusing their position, even though they represent one of the three critical success factors of the investigation.

In conclusion, process management has evolved from the observation and analysis of simple manufacturing actions into an approach that enables us a complete mapping of complex organizational systems within virtual environments in which it is possible to modify the existing process and then observe the triggered changes and their consequences. Solutions like this meet the trend of real-time process capturing, monitoring and modification as part of a process management system, by introducing parallel environments that provide us with ability to undertake a critical comparison between the launched simulation and an ongoing real-life process.

Acknowledgments

This research has been financed by the Slovenian Research Agency ARRS, Young researcher programme, ARRS-SP-2784/13. Creative Core FIS-NM-3330-13-500033 'Simulations' project funded by the European Union, the European Regional Development Fund. The operation is carried out within the framework of the Operational Programme for Strengthening Regional Development Potentials for the period 2007–2013, Development Priority 1: Competitiveness and Research Excellence, Priority Guideline 1.1: Improving the Competitive Skills and Research Excellence.

References

Agrež, Jernej / Damij, Nadja: "A Layer-Based, Matric Oriented Business Process Simulation Solution." *Proceedings of the 7th European Computing Conference*, WSEAS, Dubrovnik, pp. 167–172, 2013

Allwayer, Thomas: *BPMN 2.0*. Norderstedt, Germany: Books on demand, 2010.

Becker, Jőrg / Kugeler, Martin, Rosseman, Michael: *Process Management: A Guide for the Design of Business Processes*. Berlin, Germany: Springer, 2003.

Benner, J. Mary / Tushman, L. Michael: "Exploitation, Exploration, and Process Management: The Productivity Dilemma Revisited." *The Academy of Management Review*, 28(2), 2001, pp. 238–256.

Bieberstein, Norbert / Laird, Robert / Jones, Keith / Mitra, Tilak: *Executing SOA: A Practical Guide for the Service-Oriented Architect*. Boston, MA: Addison-Wesley Professional, 2008.

Bobbio, Andrea: *System Modeling with Petri Nets*, 1990, downloaded April, 10th, 2013, from ftp://95.31.13.230/mirea/6/os-2010/petri/Petri%203D/Petri%203D/%D0%9A%D0%BD%D0%B8%D0%B3%D0%B0/miopetrinet.pdf.

Boxwell, J. Robert: *Benchmarking for competitive advantage*. New York, McGraw-Hill, 1994.

Brunson, Karin Holmblad: "Some Effects of Fayolism." *International Studies of Management & Organization*, 38(1), 2008, pp. 30–47.

Cernaushas, Deborah / Tartantino Anthony: "Operational Risk Management with Process Control and Business Process Modeling. *The Journal of Operational Risk*, 4(2), 2009, pp. 3–17.

Chen, Peng / Zhang, Jiquan / Jiang, Xinyu / Liu, Xingpeng / Bao, Yulong / Sun, Yingyue: "Scenario Simulation-Based Assessment of Trip Difficulty for Urban Residents under Rainstorm Waterlogging." *International Journal of Environmental Research and Public Health*, 9(1), 2013, pp. 2058–2074.

Chung, H. Chen: "It Is the Process: A Philosophical Foundation for Quality Management." *Total Quality Management*, 10(2), 2009, pp. 187–197.

Cohen, Oded: *24 – Managing Day to Day Operations*. New York, NY: McGraw-Hill, 2010.

Damij, Nadja: "Business Process Modelling Using Diagrammatic and Tabular Techniques." *Business Process Management Journal*, 13(1), 2007, pp. 70–90.

Damij, Talib: "An Object Oriented Methodology for Information Systems Development and Business Process Reengineering." *Journal of Object-Oriented Programming*, 13(4), 2000, pp. 23–34.

Davenport, H. Thomas: "The Coming Commoditization of Processes." *Harvard Business Review*, 2005, http://hbr.org/2005/06/the-coming-commoditization-of-processes/ar/1, downloaded October 22nd, 2013.

Eckes, George: *General Electric's Six Sigma Revolution: How General Electric and Others Turned Process into Profits*. Danvers, MA: John Wiley & Sons, 2001.

Fujimoto, Takahiro: *The Evolution of a Manufacturing System at Toyota*. New York, NY: Oxford University Press, 1999.

Gantt, H. Laurence: *Work, Wages, and Profits*. New York, NY: Engineering Magazine Co, 1913.

George, S. Claude: *The History of Management Thought*. Newark, NJ: Prentice Hall, 1968.

Gong, Ruinan / Li, Qing / Ning, Ke / Chen, Yuliu / O`Sullivan, David: "Business Process Collaboration Using Semantic Interoperability: Review and Framework." *Semantic web – ASWC 2006 Proceedings*, lecture notes in computer science; http://citeseerx.ist.psu.edu/viewdoc/download?doi= 10.1.1.100.8485&rep=rep1&type=pdf, downloaded October 22nd, 2013.

Greasley, Andrew: "Using Business-Process Simulation within a Business-Process Reengineering Approach. *Business Process Management Journal*, 9(4), 2003, pp. 408–420.

Grover, Varun / Kettinger, J. William: *Process Think: Winning Perspectives for Business Change in the Information Age*. Hershey, PA: Idea Group Inc, 2000.

Gupta, Aditya: *Babur and Humayun: Modern Learning Organisation*. Raleigh, NC: Lulu Press, Inc, 2009.

Hammer, Michael / Champy, James: *Reengineering the Corporation, A Manifesto for Business Revolution*. New York, NY: HarperCollins, 1993/2009,,https://www.google.si/url?sa=t&rct=j&q=&esrc=s&source =web&cd=1&cad=rja&sqi=2&ved=0CC0QFjAA&url=http%3A%2F %2Fcs5852.userapi.com%2Fu11728334%2Fdocs%2F8425ed172b16 %2FReengineering_The_Corporation_383831.pdf&ei=554PUam6Boff sgaX8oHADQ&usg=AFQjCNFgZDqAjPbSLaDZLUlqNFBGcY-kwg& bvm=bv.41867550,d.Yms, downloaded October 22nd, 2013.

Han, Seungwok / Young Hee Yong: "Petri Net-Based Context Modeling for Context-Aware Systems. *The Artificial Intelligence Review*, 37(1), 2012, pp. 43–67.

Harrington, H. James: *Business Process Improvement: The Breakthrough Strategy for Total Quality, Productivity, and Competitiveness*. New York, NY: McGraw-Hill, 1991.

Hastings, R. Melissa / Funk, H. Kenneth: "Improving the Navigation and Information Integration of Complex Process Models: A Case Study Using IDEF0." *IIE Annual Conference Proceedings*, pp. 1172–1177, 2008.

Herrmann, W. Jeffrey: "The Perspectives of Taylor, Gantt, and Johnson: How to Improve Production Scheduling." *European Journal of Operational Research*, 16(3), pp. 243–254, 2010.

Hűffner, Tapio: *The BPM Productivity Model – Towards a Framework for Assessing the Business Process Maturity of Organisations*, 2004, http://books.google.si/books?id=BuXMmUiGNLcC&printsec=frontcover&dq=An+Overview+of+the+Business+Process+Maturity+Model&hl=sl&sa=X&ei=6zMEUcTbBc_ItAbzvoHoDg&redir_esc=y#v=onepage&q=An%20Overview%20of%20the%20Business%20Process%20Maturity%20Model&f=false, downloaded October 22nd, 2013.

IDEF3: Process Description Capture Method, http://www.idef.com/IDEF3.htm, downloaded October 22nd, 2013.

Jones, V. Cristopher: "The Three-Dimensional Gantt Chart." *Operations Research*, 36(6), 1988, pp. 891–902.

Kacprzak, Marek / Kaczmarczyk, Andrzej: "Verification of Integrated IDEF Models." *Journal of Intelligent Manufacturing*, 17(1), 2006, pp. 585–596.

Kano, Makoto / Koide, Akio / Te-Kai, Liu / Ramachadran, Bala.: Analysis and Simulation of Business Solutions in a Service-Oriented Architecture. *IBM Systems Journal*, 44(4), 2005, pp. 669–690.

Kim, Hee-Wong / Kim, Young-Gul.: "Dynamic Process Modeling for BPR: A Computerized Simulation Approach." *Information and Management*, 32(1), 2007, pp. 1–13.

Kim, Cheol-Han / Yim, D.-S.: Weston, H. Richard: "An Integrated Use of IDEF0, IDEF3 and Petri Net Methods in Support of Business Process Modeling." *Proceedings of the Institution of Mechanical Engineers*, 215(4), 2001, pp. 317–329.

Lampert, M. Douglas / Cooper, C. Martha: "Issues in Supply Chain Management." *Industrial Marketing Management*, 29, 2000, pp. 65–83.

Lerner, S. Barbara / Christov, Stefan / Osterweil, J. Leon / Bendraou, Reda / Kannengiesser, Udo / Wise, Alexander: "Exception Handling Patterns for Process Modeling." *IEEE Transactions on Software Engineering*, 36(2), 2010, pp. 162–183.

Linthicum, S. David: *Enterprise Application Integration*. Boston, MA: Addison-Wesley, 2003.

Maruster, Laura / van Beest, R.T.P. Nick: "Redesigning Business Processes: A Methodology Based on Simulation and Process Mining Techniques." *Knowledge Information Systems*, 21(1), 2009, pp. 267–297.

McDowell, Linda: "Life without Father and Ford: The New Gender Order of Post-Fordism." *Transactions of the Institute of British Geographers,* New Series, 16(4), 1991, pp. 400–419.

Nanda, K. Jayanta: *Management Thought.* New Delhi, India: Sarup & Sons, 2006, http://books.google.si/books?id=VtjTyhi7g4QC&printsec =frontcover&dq=Management+Thought&hl=sl&sa=X&ei=y4UPUcG nHsGytAbfg4DgCA&redir_esc=y, downloaded October 22nd, 2013.

Pankaja, P. Kumar: "Effective Use of Gantt Chart for Managing Large Scale Projects." *Cost Engineering,* 47(7), 2005, pp 14–21.

Paulk, C. Mark / Curtis, Bill / Chrissis, B. Mary / Weber, Charlie: *Capability Maturity Model for Software, version 1.1., Technical Report CMU/ SEI-93-TR-024,* February 1993, https://www.google.si/url?sa=t&rct= j&q=&esrc=s&source=web&cd=1&cad=rja&ved=0CCsQFjAA& url=http%3A%2F%2Fwww.sei.cmu.edu%2Flibrary%2Fabstracts%2F reports%2F93tr024.cfm&ei=qqUPUfTNI4jNsgbQrIG4Bg&usg=AFQj CNHHJ-XIjMDguRIpIEX94A7vkbX8LA&bvm=bv.41867550,d.Yms, downloaded October 22nd, 2013.

Peleg, Mor / Rubin, Daniel / Altman, B. Russ: "Using Petri Net Tools to Study Properties and Dynamics of Biological Systems." *Journal of the American Medical Informatics Association,* 12(2), 2005, pp. 181–99.

Plaila, Antonella / Carrie, Allan: "Application and Assessment of IDEF3 – Process Flow Description Capture Method." *International Journal of Operations & Production Management,* 63(1), 1995, http://140.118.1.131/ teaching/BPE%20under%202005/IDEF3%20paper1.pdf, downloaded October 22nd, 2013.

Plenkiewicz, Peter: *The Executive Guide to Business Process Management: How to Maximize "Lean" and "Six Sigma" Synergy and See Your Bottom Line Explode.* Bloomington, IN: iUniverse, 2010.

Pourshahid, Alireza / Amyot, Daniel, Peyton, Liam, Ghanavati, Sepideh, Chen, Pengfei, Weiss, Michael, Forster, J. Alan: *Business Process Management with the User Requirements Notation.* Electronic Commerce Research, 9(4), 2009, pp. 269–316.

Porter, E. Michael: *Competitive Advantage.* New York: The Free Press, 1985.

Powell, C. Thomas: *Total Quality Management as Competitive Advantage: A Review and Empirical Study. Strategic Management Journal*, 16(1), 1995, pp. 15–37.

Rand, K. Graham: "Critical Chain: The Theory of Constraints Applied to Project Management." *International Journal of Project Management*, 18(1), 2000, pp. 173–177.

Recker, Jan / Indulska, Marta / Rosemann, Michael / Green, Peter: "Business Process Modeling – A Comparative Analysis." *Journal of the Association for Information Systems*, 10(4), 2006, pp. 333–363.

Reeves, A. Carol / Bednar, D. Allan.: "Defining Quality: Alternatives and Implications. *Academy of Management Review*, 18(1), 1994, pp. 419–445.

Smith, Howard / Fingar, Peter: *Business Process Management: The Third Wave*. Tampa, FL: Meghan-Kiffer Press, 2002. Downloaded from http://uece-ees-t3-tcc.googlecode.com/svn/trunk/refs/BPM-3Waves.pdf, downloaded October 22nd, 2013

Taylor, W. Frederick: *The Principles of Scientific Management*, 1911, https://www.google.si/url?sa=t&rct=j&q=&esrc=s&source=web&cd=1&cad=rja&ved=0CCgQFjAA&url=http%3A%2F%2Fwww.enebooks.com%2Fdata%2FJK82mxJBHsrAsdHqQvsK%2F2010-01-19 %2F1263902254.pdf&ei=fYEPUZDmN8TMtAbK24DgBw&usg=AFQjCNE61fWfqnQgM-afIoCj1Aie1p6H4Q, downloaded October 22nd, 2013.

Tolliday, Steven / Zeitlin, Jonathan: *Between Fordism and Flexibility: The Automobile Industry and Its Workers – Past, Present and Future*. New York: St. Martin's Press, 1987, http://library.fes.de/afs/derivat_pdf/jportal_derivate_00020783/afs-1988-153.pdf, downloaded October 22nd, 2013.

Trkman, Peter: "The Critical Success Factors of Business Process Management." *International Journal of Information Management*, 30(2), 2010, pp. 125–134.

Umble, J. Elisabeth / Haft, R. Ronald / Umble, M. Michael: "Enterprise Resource Planning: Implementation Procedures and Critical Success Factors." *European Journal of Operational Research*, 146, 2003, pp. 241–257.

van der Aalst, Wil: "The Application of Petri Nets to Workflow Management." *Journal of Circuits, Systems and Computers*, 8(1), 1998, pp. 21–66.

van der Aalst, M. P. Wil / Dumas, Marlon / Hofstede, H. M. Arthur / Wohed, Petia: *Pattern-Based Analysis of BPML (and WSCI). QUT Technical report, FIT-TR-2002–05*, Brisbane: Queensland University of Technology, 2002, http://citeseerx.ist.psu.edu/viewdoc/download?doi=10.1.1.11.7424&rep=rep1&type=pdf, downloaded October 22nd, 2013.

van der Aalst, M. P. Wil / Hofstede, H. M. Arthur / Weske, Mathias: "Business Process Management: A Survey." *Proceedings of the 1st International Conference on Business Process Management*, vol. 2678 of LNCS, 2003, pp. 1–12.

Wilson, M. James: "Gantt Charts: A Centenary Appreciation." *European Journal of Operational Research*, 149(1), 2003, pp. 430–437.

Womack, P. James / Jones, T. Daniel: *Lean Thinking: Banish Waste and Create Wealth in Your Corporation*. New York, NY: Simon and Schuster, 2003.

Yin, Zhan'e / Xu, Shiyuan / Yin, Jie / Wang, Jiahong: "Community-Based Scenario Modelling and Disaster Risk Assessment of Urban Rainstorm Waterlogging." *Journal of Geographical Sciences*, 21(2), 2010, pp. 274–284.

Renato Barisic
Algebra University College for Applied Computer Engineering, Zagreb, Croatia

Secondary School Students and Printed Textbooks

Abstract: Modern information and communication technologies suited to be used in the educational process have to bridge the gap between the desires of today's students for modern educational content and compulsory literature in the form of printed textbooks. This paper presents the results of research on use of printed textbooks in the Humanities, Social Sciences, Natural Sciences and Engineering in the third and fourth grade of secondary school. The survey was conducted among 806 students from 21 secondary schools from 9 Croatian counties. An analysis of research on the use of printed textbooks in the final years of secondary school shows that a significant number of textbooks are used on a small scale during the day at school and even to a lesser extent during independent work at home. The aim of this paper is to highlight the need to find alternative and complementary solutions whose application should modernize the educational process and present courses to students in an attractive and motivating way on a variety of devices that today's students have at home, at school and on the move.

Keywords: content, education, information, student, textbook

1. Introduction

The daily creation and sharing of unlimited amounts of information is not possible with traditional printed resources due to the slowness of their production and the inability to change content in the light of new knowledge creation and technological achievements.

In the last decade, several authors have address the issue of printed textbooks as everyday teaching resources by analyzing the attributes of efficiency, convenience, rationality and expediency (Brusilovsky, Ahn & Rasmussen 2010, Cauthen & Halpin 2010, Donovan & Bransford 2005, Mayer 2005).

Using digital content provides flexibility to individualized learning. It increases motivation and students' self-esteem because it helps them to adopt their own knowledge. However, use of a computer itself does not necessarily mean that students will develop the abilities of divergent thinking, creativity, cooperation, responsibility, decision-making, democratic behavior, etc. (Spanovic 2010, p. 468).

The application of multimedia in education, i.e. in the teaching process, can contribute to the technological and audio-visual attractiveness and thus adapt the educational process to the requirements of modern students. Multimedia files give another dimension to the data. They allow users to find out more on a specific subject and explore it in more detail. This can be detailed information of the subject itself or it can contain pictures, videos or other documents related to that subject (Barisic 2011, p. 155).

Even if you do not raise doubts about the accuracy, completeness or timeliness of the classic printed textbooks, we need to rethink whether a teaching aid in that form is suitable for the education of the modern, technology-minded, younger generations – and consider whether modern tech-savvy teachers would use classic printed teaching tools as their first choice for the high-quality transmission of knowledge in educational institutions of 21st century? Are there alternatives or complements, i.e., are there opportunities, methods and systems that can meet the classroom demands and desires of today's students and which will motivate them to learn and explore?

2. Methodology

2.1 Method

The research was conducted during the period from 22nd November 2012 to 13th May 2013 in 21 secondary schools in 9 Croatian counties. A survey was the selected data collection method.

Prior to conducting the survey permission was sought from the responsible persons: the principal, school counselor, psychologist or teacher. The survey was carried out in groups, on a voluntary basis, with one or two classes that were present in the classroom at the same time. At the beginning of the survey the interviewer demonstrated the paper format questionnaire to students and they were given instructions for filling it out. The interviewer emphasized that the survey was completely anonymous and did not collect any personal or school data. The time in which to fill in the questionnaire was limited to 10 minutes.

2.2 Instrument

The data collection instrument was a questionnaire. The questionnaire completed by the students consisted of both general questions and specific questions about the use of printed textbooks and digital content.

The general questions were about age, gender, type of school, and the direction of the class are primarily used for the analysis and presentation of the structure of the respondents according to various criteria. Given that the target sample was students in the third and fourth grade of secondary school, the question about respondents' age offered a choice between 13 and 19. The question about gender could be responded by circling M for male or F for female. When asked about the type of school, the students could respond with T for technical school or with G for gymnasium. The question about the direction of education was set up as an open question which could be answered by free writing. The last question was a general question about the current grade with possible answers 1 to 4. It is axiomatic that the target population was fourth grade, and third grade at times. Still, there was an option of circling first grade or second grade if someone from the lower grade appeared.

Questions about the use of printed textbooks and digital content were presented as a closed set of multiple choice questions. A question about the use of printed textbooks during the schooling was constructed in the form of a table where the columns highlight three main divisions: subject, at school, at home. In the subject column was a list of subjects in the Humanities (Croatian, foreign languages, History, Religion, Ethics), Social Sciences (Politics and Economy), Natural Sciences (Mathematics, Physics, Geography) and Engineering (Computer Science, Information Science). In the group of columns at school and at home, there were subdivisions which offered intensities: never, rarely, often or always. With this approach the students were able to immediately designate the usage intensity of printed textbooks at school and at home for one course. Below the table were two further questions about use of digital content at school and during independent work at home and they offered the possible answers: never, rarely, often and very often.

2.3 Sample

The questionnaire was answered by 806 students. There were no invalid questionnaires and possibly unanswered questions are, during data enrolment, set to 0 or X indicating no response and at figures that are shown as a generally accepted abbreviation „n/a", which means no answer. Such an approach provides a number of students who did not answer a particular question.

Given that these were secondary school students, both third grade (114) and fourth grade (692) respondents are aged between 16 and 19. The sample included both male (717) and female (89) students. The technical school was attended by 760 students in several technical directions and the gymnasium was attended by 46 students in the general and mathematics direction.

The demographic of respondents by age, gender, type of school and grade are visible in Figures 1, 2, 3 and 4.

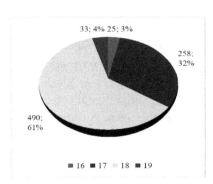

Fig. 1: Age

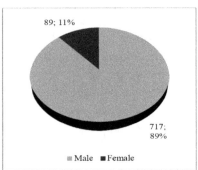

Fig. 2: Gender

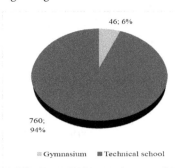

Fig. 3: Type of school

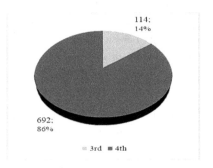

Fig. 4: Grade

3. Results

3.1 Use of Printed Textbooks at School

Data on use of printed textbooks at school that are otherwise presented and analyzed in groups according to the sciences to which they belong, in this section will be displayed in one place regardless of the scientific field, in order to monitor the use or non-use of textbooks in each subject. The chart and accompanying tables are shown in Figures 5 and 6.

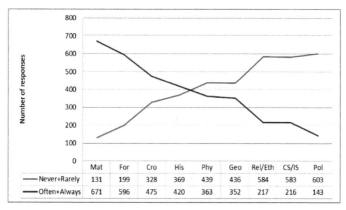

	Mat	For	Cro	His	Phy	Geo	Rel/Eth	CS/IS	Pol
Never+Rarely	131	199	328	369	439	436	584	583	603
Often+Always	671	596	475	420	363	352	217	216	143

Fig. 5: Use of printed textbooks at school – number of responses

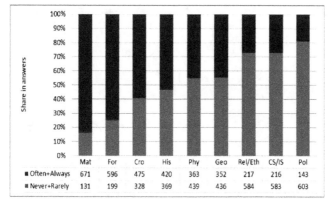

	Mat	For	Cro	His	Phy	Geo	Rel/Eth	CS/IS	Pol
Often+Always	671	596	475	420	363	352	217	216	143
Never+Rarely	131	199	328	369	439	436	584	583	603

Fig. 6: Use of printed textbooks at school – share in answers

3.2 Use of Printed Textbooks at Home

Data on use of printed textbooks at home that are otherwise presented and analyzed in groups according to the sciences to which they belong, in this section will be displayed in one place regardless of the scientific field, in order to monitor the use or non-use of textbooks in each subject. The chart and accompanying tables are shown Figures 7 and 8.

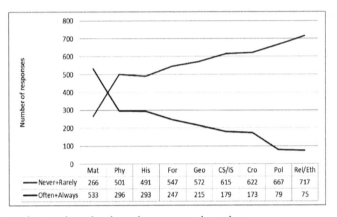

	Mat	Phy	His	For	Geo	CS/IS	Cro	Pol	Rel/Eth
Never+Rarely	266	501	491	547	572	615	622	667	717
Often+Always	533	296	293	247	215	179	173	79	75

Fig. 7: Use of printed textbooks at home – number of responses

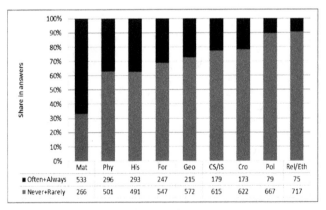

	Mat	Phy	His	For	Geo	CS/IS	Cro	Pol	Rel/Eth
Often+Always	533	296	293	247	215	179	173	79	75
Never+Rarely	266	501	491	547	572	615	622	667	717

Fig. 8: Use of printed textbooks at home – share in answers

3.3 Use of Digital Content at School

Data and analysis of the given answers about the usage of digital content (presentation, e-learning content, interactive content, computer simulations, quizzes, games, .pdf, .doc and .docx documents, etc.) during the day at school are shown in Figures 9 and 10 and accompanying tables.

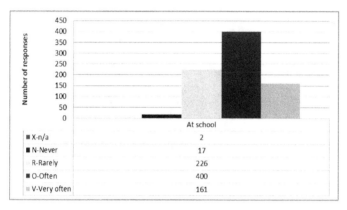

Fig. 9: Use of digital content at school – number of responses

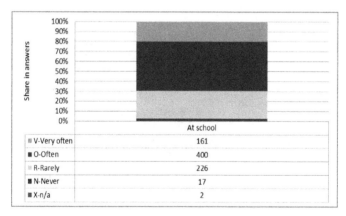

Fig. 10: Use of digital content at school – share in answers

3.4 Use of Digital Content at Home

Data and analysis of the given answers about the usage of digital content (presentation, e-learning content, interactive content, computer simulations, quizzes, games, .pdf, .doc and .docx documents, etc.) during independent work at home is shown in Figures 11 and 12 and accompanying tables.

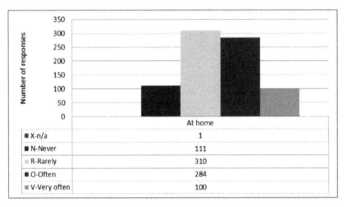

	At home
X-n/a	1
N-Never	111
R-Rarely	310
O-Often	284
V-Very often	100

Fig. 11: Use of digital content at home – number of responses

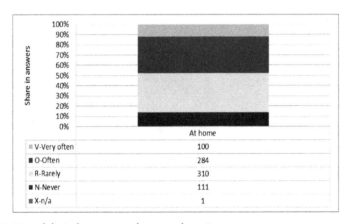

	At home
V-Very often	100
O-Often	284
R-Rarely	310
N-Never	111
X-n/a	1

Fig. 12: Use of digital content at home – share in answers

4. Conclusion

The results of the surveys conducted among students in the third and fourth grades of secondary schools on their use of printed textbooks from 9 subjects in the Humanities, Social Sciences, Natural Sciences and Engineering show that textbooks in only 4 of 9 courses are regularly used in the classroom at school, and only 1 of 9 used regularly during independent work at home. Research has shown that there are a significant number of subjects for which the classical printed textbooks are very little used and some hardly used. This especially applies to use of textbooks at home, but it is evident that the usage at school is not, for the majority of analyzed subjects, much better. These data indicate that students are not motivated and do not want to significantly use printed textbooks and that teachers do not insist on their use at schools, and even at home.

Analysis of digital content use has shown that they digital content is extensively used during the day at school and during students' independent work at home. It is obvious that both the teachers and (especially) modern generations of students have already adopted electronic communication and the presentation of teaching content assisted by digital content and technology as common and everyday.

References

Barisic, Renato: "Geanium – Interactive Chronological Visualization System". *Croatian Journal of Education* 13(4), 2011, pp. 151–174, ISSN: 1846–1204.

Brusilovsky, Peter / Ahn, Jae-Wook / Rasmussen, Edie: "Teaching Information Retrieval with Web-Based Interactive Visualization". *Journal of Education for Library and Information Science* 51(3), 2010, pp. 187–200, ISSN: 0748–5786.

Cauthen, Leilani / Halpin, John: *Digital Content & Learning Management Platforms*. Center for Digital Education: Folsom, 2010.

Donovan, Suzanne M. / Bransford, John D.: *How Students Learn: Science in the Classroom*. The National Academies Press: Washington, 2005.

Mayer, Richard E.: *The Cambridge Handbook of Multimedia Learning*. Cambridge University Press: Cambridge, 2005.

Spanovic, Svetlana: "Pedagogical Aspects of E-Textbooks". *Educational Sciences* 12(2), 2010, pp. 459–470.

Nadja Damij and Grezegor Majewski
Faculty of Information Studies in Novo mesto, Slovenia

Inclusion of Tacit Knowledge in the Simulation of Business Processes

Abstract: This paper investigates potential methods of including tacit knowledge into the business process simulation agenda. It identifies key characteristics of tacit knowledge and how they can relate to the business process simulation. The significant contribution of this work is that it proposes a generic approach to including tacit knowledge in the simulation of business processes. This generic approach is based on the widely-known black box technique. It distinguishes the various situations that may occur when considering the simulation of tacit knowledge.

Keywords: business process simulation, business process modeling, tacit knowledge, black box

1 Introduction

Knowledge is widely regarded as a critical asset in modern organizations (Teerajetgul and Chareonngam, 2012). It has been seen as a source of income generation and a way to gain competitive advantage in profit-oriented organizations. However, in order to achieve these goals, organizations face the challenge of properly managing their knowledge. Knowledge management can be perceived as a fundamental process for managing organizations (Bailey and Clarke 2000). This process is both technology – as well as people-dependent. Knowledge itself has been classified according to a variety of criteria. One such classification was done by Nonaka and Takeuchi (1995). This classification distinguishes explicit and tacit knowledge. The first kind can be codified easily into a form (e.g. written or electronic) which can be "transferred" to others. Tacit knowledge is less tangible and therefore its processes of generation and transfer are more complex.

Tacit knowledge may be perceived as a combination of education, training and real life experiences. An individual may acquire tacit knowledge such as mental models and technical skills through observation, imitation and practice (Teerajetgul & Chareonngam 2012). Furthermore, tacit knowledge can be either perceived as such because of intrinsic difficulties in sharing it (e.g. amount, experiences that have to be lived through) or because the person, group or organization bearing it may be not fully aware of it. Polanyi (1966) provides an insight into the essence of tacit knowledge in the words "We know more than we can tell". Further clarification of these words can be in the form of examples such as riding a bicycle or swimming. Once these activities are learnt it is difficult relay the knowledge associated with them. They may however be learnt by observing and experiencing them. Tacit and explicit knowledge are, however, very closely connected to each other and the distinction between them must be treated with caution. Tacit knowledge may be possessed by itself; however explicit knowledge must "rely on being tacitly understood and applied" (Senker 1995, p. 426).

As the person, group or organization progresses through real-life experiences it acquires a lot of information. Some of this information is acquired unintentionally. The brain is known to record and store experiences from the senses; however not all of these experiences are fully processed. Some of the experiences and information may be quickly and effortlessly recalled, while others are difficult to remember. They may however be recalled in special circumstances, when there is a vital need for that. Another example of tacit knowledge that may exist on the edge of awareness is daily routines. These are almost-mechanical activities that (although they may differ in nature depending on position) are performed in a similar way across the organization from a simple manual worker to a top executive. Quite often, a given person, when asked how a given goal or task was achieved, is unable to give a detailed response. This truth is a common fact experienced by any business process analyst. Moreover tacit knowledge is usually built on top of experiences over many years. In order to effectively generate business knowledge, either explicit or tacit, it is a necessity for business leaders to imitate the experiences that built that knowledge in the first place. It is a common truth that business process simulation and modeling is an effective way to analyze even time-consuming business processes that can span a wide timeframe. In other words, business simulations provide "a field of interaction where multiyear experiences are created in compressed timeframes" (Lefebvre 2011). In this view business process simulation serves as a tool that can be utilized to gain insight into "not fully recognized" business processes as well as into a tacit knowledge transfer method that mimics lifelong experiences.

2 Literature Review

Nowadays, organizations have to operate in unknown environments which, moreover, change rapidly. Decisions in such environments are often guided by intuition and lifelong experience. They often have far-reaching consequences and need to be taken in a very limited timeframe. There is a crucial need to understand the nature and role of tacit knowledge, as well as possible ways to disseminate it both within the organization and externally. One way to achieve this is from a process perspective, which is "concerned with the accumulation of implicit knowledge acquired over time in organizational processes" (Venkitachalam & Busch 2012, p. 356). This perspective may be, however, insufficient to adequately comprehend all of the intangible dynamics intrinsic to tacit knowledge generation, adoption and diffusion. Apart from that, tacit knowledge is recognized as highly contextual (Busch 2008). Moreover its transfer, interpretation and application requires multiple stakeholders. Therefore discussing only what tacit knowledge is, or undertaking a pure investigation of its features, should have lower priority (in both scholarship as well as business dispute) than examining we may make better use of tacit knowledge (Venkitachalam & Busch 2012, p. 357).

There is a crucial need for the clarification and understanding of tacit knowledge's significance and potential application in certain knowledge management domains. Some of these domains include: the role of tacit knowledge in organizational learning; tacit knowledge codification and transfer techniques; the influence of tacit knowledge on intellectual capital; the use of tacit knowledge in communities of practice; the group aspect of tacit knowledge (knowledge networks and teams); and the relation of tacit knowledge to technology.

Modern organizations have realized the need and advantages of investments in developing employee capabilities as part of their training and work environment. However, the "influence of employee profile in the use of tacit knowledge is not adequately evident in the literature" (Venkitachalam & Busch 2012, p. 364).

The knowledge management discipline has in the past focused too much on technology (e.g. expert systems) and therefore the human factor was often overlooked. This approach gained a significant amount of criticism as it focused its attention on the technology itself and the design of e.g. "intelligent machines" using, for instance, artificial intelligence (AI) techniques, which were often inadequate in meeting real world challenges. Instead, knowledge management advocates the design of tools, techniques and technologies that augment human capabilities. Apart from that, there are a lot of studies that examined the meaning and definition of tacit knowledge but comparatively very few studies which have analyzing tacit knowledge (Venkitachalam & Busch 2012, p. 364).

Individual vs. Group Tacit Knowledge

Knowledge (both explicit and tacit) can be related to and analyzed at the level of individual or group (community or organization) (Nonaka & Takeuchi 1995, Merx-Chemin & Nijhof 2005, Teerajetgul & Chareonngam 2008, Venkitachalam & Busch 2012). It is expected that at the individual level knowledge will mainly consist of tacit knowledge, which is not typically articulated but may be codified depending upon the circumstances. At the group level one can expect a greater sharing of explicit knowledge. This is quite obvious given the fact that knowledge-sharing processes (which require some sort of codification) occur more often at the group level. Some authors regard procedural knowledge as a form of tacit knowledge (Colonia-Willner 2004, Sternberg & Hedlund 2002, Bossen & Dalsgaard 2005). This sort of knowledge is usually used to carry out daily activities and is relevant to the person making use of it (individual level). On the organizational level this type of knowledge becomes a practical intelligence to the organization (Venkitachalam & Busch 2012).

The role of groups, teams, communities, networks in the modern organizations and their approach to tacit knowledge is of crucial importance (Jorgensen 2004). There are a variety of factors that influence the knowledge-sharing processes within teams: e.g. trust, sense of belonging, composition of teams, culture and technology. Another important thing to remember is that knowledge, and in particular tacit knowledge, is sticky by nature (Szulanski 2003). This indicates that the more valuable the (tacit) knowledge, the less likely the individual, group, team, community or society is to share or transfer it out. In this view sharing or transfering such knowledge may mean losing competitive advantage over other individuals, groups, teams or organizations. Some authors reveal that in some cases the sharing of knowledge (and in particular tacit knowledge) causes the individual or team to become less important to the organization (Desouza & Evaristo 2004). Moreover, the more time and resources that were devoted to generating such knowledge, the less likely its sharing or transfer is to occur.

3 Black-Box (BB) Approach

As explained in the previous sections, tacit knowledge may, due to its nature, pose difficulties while being included in the business process simulation. Moreover the characteristics of the tacit knowledge may differ from one industry to another and from one type of organization to another. In this paper the authors would like to propose a generic approach that can be utilized regardless of the type of industry, organization or the particular characteristics of the tacit knowledge. In order to provide such a generic solution it is necessary to realize that tacit knowledge is very closely related to the individual, group or community and it is very difficult to separate it from the underlying base – "when recognizing the very contextual nature of tacit knowledge, it makes little sense to attribute properties to knowledge that does not exist outside human consciousness" (Venkitachalam & Busch 2012, p. 361). Therefore the first step in the inclusion of tacit knowledge in the business process simulation is the identification of the resource (e.g. individual, group or community) that possesses a tacit knowledge which allows higher productivity. In other words, if a given individual, group or community achieves better results than the others it may be an indication that it possesses a strategic tacit knowledge, which may increase the overall productivity. Inclusion of this tacit knowledge may provide a greater insight into the internal process-flow. This section will further investigate a potential solution to how to include tacit knowledge in the business process simulation. It will describe an approach originating from the well-known black-box concept.

Black-box is a term in computer science which denotes that it is possible to observe, measure and analyze input(s) and output(s) of a given system, device, program, object, module or application; however it is not possible to have an insight into the internal mechanics of the process behind "translating" input(s) into output(s) (Delinchant et al. 2007, p. 369). The black-box approach, due to its characteristics, may establish a very good generic starting point for the inclusion of tacit knowledge into the business process simulation. As explained previously, tacit knowledge is intrinsically related to an individual, group or community. Therefore it may be impossible to measure its impact on business processes directly, but it may be possible to measure the difference in how the input(s) are "translated" into output(s) in two distinct cases. The first case is when a given resource (individual, group or community) that possesses the tacit knowledge is present (i.e. the business process has the full benefit of the tacit knowledge or, rather, the resource that possesses it). The second case occurs when the resource possessing the tacit knowledge is artificially removed from the business process or replaced with a resource which only possesses a generic explicit knowledge. Process analysts can easily compare the output(s) of both cases and deduce how important the tacit knowledge is to the successful completion of the business process, how much time or resources can be spared with the use of this particular tacit knowledge and how well the input(s) will be translated into desired output(s). Such an analysis is relatively easy to carry out and should bear close similarities to the common tasks performed by process analysts. Moreover its ease of use meets the criteria for a generic approach (i.e. one that can be used in any situation with relatively low effort/cost). Once the information obtained through this step is available, the process analyst can decide whether there is a need to further investigate what particular tacit knowledge may be involved in a particular business process.

In some cases the reason for knowledge to remain in a tacit state might be due to the cost. "Whether a particular bit of knowledge is in principle articulable or necessarily tacit is not a relevant question in most behavioral situation. Rather, the question is whether the costs associated with the obstacles to articulat[ion] are sufficiently high so that the knowledge in fact remains tacit" (Nelson & Winter 1982, p. 82). At this point, the process analyst should calculate the costs associated with the obstacles related to the articulation of the tacit knowledge. Should these costs be higher than the potential gains (as observed in the previous step) it would be advisable to simply disregard the tacit knowledge in the simulated process(es).

However it is important to remember that this situation may change in the future (i.e. the costs of articulation of tacit knowledge may be lower than the potential gains); therefore it is sensible to also monitor the changes in the process(es) and, should such changes occur, adjust the analysis by including tacit knowledge.

It is a common truth that tacit knowledge differs from industry to industry and from one organization to another. The black-box approach allows us to disregard such differences and assess whether the inclusion of tacit knowledge in the business process simulation is an economically viable option. The next section of this paper will provide an insight into the post black-box analysis.

4 Post Black-Box Analysis

Once the black-box approach analysis of tacit knowledge in business process(es) is concluded it may be reasonable to further analyze the whole situation. The previous section hinted at some of the most important questions that need to be answered (e.g. whether it is economically feasible to investigate the articulation of tacit knowledge). At this point it is necessary to realize that the proportion and impact of tacit knowledge on a business process may be greatly influenced by the nature of the business process as well as the industry type or the organization's profile. In the case of individuals who are mainly involved in manual labor (e.g. the manufacturing industry, mining or agriculture) it is possible to state that tacit knowledge (although still important) may make a relatively small contribution towards the final outcome of the given process in which this individual is involved. This situation radically changes in the case of individuals who are mainly involved in cognitive labour (e.g. software programming, research and development, professional services).

It is possible to state that the replacement (as suggested by the black-box approach presented previously) of a manual laborer with extensive tacit knowledge with another one that possesses only generic explicit knowledge or training in the field may only result in slight delays or output(s) of slightly lower quality. This statement however would be wholly wrong in the case of the replacement, for example, of an experienced software programmer with years of experience with another one possessing only generic training. The difference in the productivity in this case may be as much as twenty times more (Atwood 2004). On the other hand, manual workers and corresponding manual processes are more common. Therefore it is possible to state that even a slight improvement in such processes may be multiplied (with relatively more ease than in the case of predominantly cognitive processes) by the numerous instances in such a process is likely to occur. In other words, the inclusion of tacit knowledge in predominantly manual processes that occur very frequently may result in considerably better outputs or greater savings that can be observed on a mass scale. Predominantly cognitive processes may not be able to reach such a mass scale, given the lower number of workers involved in them. Moreover, predominantly manual processes usually have a lower cost associated with articulating tacit knowledge so that it is available to other workers, when compared with highly cognitive processes.

At this point (having the information presented in the previous section) it is feasible to reconsider the economic side of tacit knowledge and the nature of the processes influenced by it. A process analyst should investigate how often a given process will occur in the real world and then re-evaluate (using the black-box approach), whether it is feasible to include tacit knowledge in further analysis. It is necessary to remember that any potential benefits may be multiplied by the number of occurrences of a given process in the real world.

Business process simulation can further aid the processes of tacit knowledge creation and transfer. As explained previously, business simulation offers a field of interaction where "multiyear experiences are created in compressed timeframes" (Lefebvre 2011). In this view the process analyst provides an artificial environment to the process stakeholders, when they can observe the process (input[s], output[s], decision points, etc.). These stakeholders can learn from this observation in a similar way that they would learn from real-world experiences. It is however important to remember that the business processes in such analysis are an approximation of real-world business processes. They will never carry one hundred percent of the information that the real-world setting would convey. Nonetheless this may be a cheaper, less time-consuming option by which to learn the tacit knowledge other people gained through lifelong experiences. This option however should be available only once the previous steps were accomplished.

This section of the paper covered the potential post black-box analysis of tacit knowledge in business process simulation. It distinguished potential differences between tacit knowledge in mainly manual and predominantly cognitive processes. After that it suggested revisiting the comparison of potential costs incurred by the articulation of tacit knowledge with the benefits that may arise from the use of tacit knowledge in a given situation. At the end it provided the option of "compressing" long-lasting experiences which may involve tacit knowledge in the business process simulation; these may then be further shared with process stakeholders. The next section of this paper will focus on the conclusions of this work.

5 Conclusions and Recommendations for Further Work

This paper's major contribution to the field of business process simulation is the presentation of a generic approach which allows the inclusion of tacit knowledge into the business process simulation. An approach based on the black-box concept was investigated as the potential solution. It proved to be a viable option for investigating the impact of tacit knowledge (associated with a resource such as an individual or group) on the business process. Due to its characteristics this approach can be applied regardless of the nature of the business process, characteristics of the industry or the type of organization. Moreover it is relatively easy to be applied, and therefore can serve as a starting point for more sophisticated analyses.

Additionally, the characteristics of mainly manual and predominantly cognitive processes were presented together with their implications for tacit knowledge and process simulation. This was followed by the feasibility consideration and a potential option of utilizing business process simulation as a way of "compressing" lifelong experiences and presenting them to the business process stakeholders.

Future work could endeavor to further investigate the differences occurring in tacit knowledge depending on the industry type, organization profiles and business process characteristics. Such analysis could form part of a post black-box analysis, where the feasibility of the analysis could be further aided by greater insight into such differences. Eventually such work could result in concepts that could aid development of novel software for business process analysis, which would incorporate tacit knowledge. Currently there is no such software package available on the market.

Acknowledgments

This work is supported by Creative Core FISNM-3330-13-500033 ‚Simulations' project funded by the European Union, The European Regional Development Fund. The operation is carried out within the framework of the Operational Programme for Strengthening Regional Development Potentials for the period 2007–2013, Development Priority 1: Competitiveness and Research Excellence, Priority Guideline 1.1: Improving the Competitive Skills and Research Excellence.

References

Atwood, Jeff: "Skill Disparities in Programming." 2004. Retrieved 29.8.2013, from http://www.codinghorror.com/blog/2004/09/skill-disparities-in-programming.html

Bailey, Catherine / Clarke, Martin: "How Do Managers Use Knowledge about Knowledge Management?" *Journal of Knowledge Management*, 4(3), 2000, pp. 235–243.

Bossen, Claus / Dalsgaard, Peter: "Conceptualization and Appropriation: The Evolving Use of a Collaborative Knowledge Management System." *Proceedings of AARHUS'05*, Aarhus, Denmark, 2005, pp. 99–108.

Busch, Peter: *Tacit Knowledge in Organizational Learning*. IGI-Global Hershey: Pennsylvania, PA, 2008.

Colonia-Willner, Regina: "Self-Service Systems: New Methodology Reveals Customer Real-Time Actions During Merger." *Computers in Human Behavior*, 29(2), 2004, pp. 243–267.

Delinchant, Benoît / Duret, Denis / Estrabaut, Laurence / Huu, Gerbaud. H. N. / Du Peloux, Bertrand / Rakotoarison, Harijaona L. / Verdiere, Franck / Wurtz, Frédéric: "An Optimizer Using the Software Component Paradigm for the Optimization of Engineering Systems." *COMPEL: The International Journal for Computation and Mathematics in Electrical and Electronic Engineering*, 26(2), 2007, pp. 368–379.

Desouza, Kevin C. and Evaristo, Roberto J.: "Managing Knowledge in Distributed Projects." *Communications of the ACM*, 47(4), 2004, pp. 87–91.

Jorgensen, Bradley: "Individual and Organisational Learning: A Model for reform for public organisations." *Foresight*, 6(2), 2004, pp. 91–103.

Lefebvre, Jeffrey R.: "Simulations Accelerate Tacit Knowledge Transfer." 2011. Retrieved 25.8.2013, from http://clomedia.com/articles/view/simulations-accelerate-tacit-knowledge-transfer

Merx-Chermin, Mireille / Nijhof, Wim J.: "Factors Influencing Knowledge Creation and Innovation in an Organisation." *Journal of European Industrial Training*, 29(2), 2005, pp. 135–147.

Nelson, Richard, R. / Winter, Sidney G.: *An Evolutionary Theory of Economic Change*. Harvard University Press: Cambridge, MA, 1982.

Nonaka, Ikujiro / Takeuchi, Hirotaka: *The Knowledge-Creating Company*. Oxford University Press: New York, NY, 1995.

Polanyi, Michael: „The Logic of Tacit Inference." *Philosophy*, 41(155), 1966, pp. 1–18.

Senker, Jacqueline: "Tacit Knowledge and Models of Innovation." *Industrial and Corporate Change*, 4(2), 1995, pp. 425–447.

Sternberg, Robert, J. / Hedlund, Jennifer: "Practical Intelligence, g, and Work Psychology." *Human Performance*, 15(1/2), 2002, pp. 143–160.

Szulanski, Gabriel: *Sticky Knowledge: Barriers to Knowing in the Firm*. Sage Publications: Thousand, Oaks, CA, 2003.

Teerajetgul, Wasan / Chareonngam, Chotchai: "Tacit Knowledge Utilization in Thai Construction Projects." *Journal of Knowledge Management*, 12(1), 2012, pp. 164–174.

Venkitachalam, Krishna / Busch, Peter: "Tacit Knowledge: Review and Possible Research Directions." *Journal of Knowledge Management*, 16(2), 2012, pp. 356–371.

Jože Bučar
Faculty of Information Studies in Novo mesto, Slovenia

A Research Voucher Case Study: Web Clipping

Abstract: Web clipping deals with the acquisition of text and graphic components, and from web pages and their efficient display on a hand-held web appliance. Many such solutions already exist on the market. While they are mostly too expensive or do not provide desired functionality there is strong motivation to develop such solutions. The project is conducted in collaboration with company that manages the leading IT portal in Slovenia and produces news media. Our aim was to develop a web solution for data acquisition, to find out where, when and in what form information appears on the web and to detect user response. Process automation enables the company to collect data fast and effectively which will be crucial for future editorial and business decisions. In this paper we present an approach and implemented solutions that provide a better flexibility to users in selecting, retrieving, extracting and tracking information in publicly available publications on the web.

Keywords: web clipping, information retrieval, sentiment analysis, text mining, web mining

1 Introduction

The rise and immense extent of the web created an entirely new way to view, retrieve and share information. An enormous quantity of data is generated on the web daily. We are practically deluged by all kinds of data – scientific, medical, financial, historical, health care, demographic, business, and other. Usually, there are not enough human resources to examine this data. From this chaotic cluster of data we strive to obtain valuable information, which may significantly impact strategic decisions of businesses and individuals in the future.

Relevant information about a company, its structure, employees, activities, products, and services can occur anywhere on the web. Although such information can be either true or false, it has a significant impact on public opinion and its response. However, more and more business, sale, finance, and other companies are aware of people's opinion. An increasing number of blogs, web sites, newsgroups, forums, chat rooms, etc., has allowed people to express and aggregate their feelings about products, services, and events more intensively. It has made it possible to extract opinions regardless of whether we are looking for opinions on the candidates in upcoming elections or opinions about the holiday destination we intend to visit. As the phrase goes, "the customer is king". In the eyes of a company it is crucial to understand people's needs, feelings and satisfaction.

At the beginning of text mining activities scientists were dealing mainly with diverse forms of information retrieval and information summarization, such as abstracts and grouping of documents. Later researchers focused on information extraction. By tagging each document we can extract the content and structure from a corpus of documents. There are four basic types of elements that can be extracted from text: entities, attributes, facts, and events (Sanger and Feldman 2007). Typical text mining tasks include the classification and categorization of texts (documents), topic detection, sentiment analysis, summarization (summary) of texts, and the study of relationships between entities in the texts.

The classification of (web) texts is one of the key tasks in text mining. Automation of procedures for the purpose of classification of texts has thus become an important tool which has contributed to more efficient work. Therefore, data miners use a variety of tools and a wide range of learning algorithms such as Naïve Bayes (Lewis 1998), decision rules (Michalski 1973) and trees (Breiman, et al. 1984), regression methods (Harrell 2001), neural networks (Haykin 1994), the k-nearest neighbour algorithm (Cover & Hart 1967), the method of support vector machines (Cortes & Vapnik 1995), and others. Sentiment analysis, also known as opinion mining, is a field closely related to text analysis, computational linguistics, and natural language processing. Textual information can be categorized into facts (objective) and opinions (subjective information). The purpose of sentiment analysis is to determine the sentiment of textual material through the expression and contextual polarity of the source (Liu 2010).

In most developed countries automated monitoring of information on the web and other media is an everyday routine, since it improves distinctness, and ensures the stability and reputation of organizations. There are several successful companies offering comprehensive solutions for detecting, filtering, classifying, analysing, and informing users (Google Alerts and Web

Clipping, Web). In Slovenia the automated monitoring of information on the web is not yet widespread.

The project presented in this paper is developed in collaboration with the prominent company Nevtron & Company d.o.o. (Ljubljana, Slovenia), which holds the leading IT portal in Slovenia (Računalniške novice, Web). As an IT company they are interested in developing a web application for tracking up-to-date accurate information, and in level of importance evaluation of the results for their potential clients. The purpose is to obtain an up-to-date and accurate picture of the company's footprint, products, and services (e.g. news, articles, etc.). In addition to where, when, and in what way a certain piece of information appears, we are also interested in the importance of this information and user response. We want to know whether published news and articles were favourably accepted or not. The project is market-oriented and encourages the demand for services (organization and management with more information on the organization, product, service, etc.). Knowing what users think about an organization and its products and services has huge potential because it improves the company's future editorial policy and its strategic business decisions. The proposed solution will enhance the company's portfolio of services and hopefully the effort will contribute to penetration in international markets.

The rest of this paper is organized as follows: Section 2 introduces methodology and implementation and Section 3 describes challenges. Finally, the paper ends with Conclusions in Section 4.

2 Methodology and Implementation

The company produces a great amount of news and articles daily. They are mainly interested in the footprint of their content (or the content of their clients) on other web pages and digital media and in user feedback. In practice, the company has an agreement with partners that publish company's content on the web. However, they feel an urge to monitor their clients and partners whether they publish within agreements. The company is also curious about the opinion of readers – about their published news and its semantic content. The project is still under construction.

Figure 1 illustrates the architectural framework of our project based on user studies, and is divided into three main components:

- retrieval of unstructured text data;
- databases; and
- sentiment analysis.

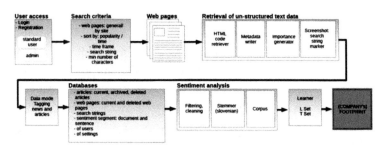

Fig. 1: Architectural framework of the web clipping application

The web application involves a group of processes that require considerable memory and processing capabilities. Therefore it runs on the company's server and its performance is dependent on the capacities and limitations of that machine.

2.1 Retrieval of Unstructured Text Data

This component finds and obtains objects within web pages and identifies hierarchical relations between them to improve the filtering process and retrieval by selecting and eliminating certain kinds of objects, such as images (Gomes et al. 2001). This phase represents the most significant of the implementation phases.

Initially we studied which of the existing search engines was most suitable to solve the problem. We chose the Google Custom Search Engine, which adjusts the search parameters to implement specified solutions. We developed a module for automatic identification which captures text from web sources and records it into the database:

- Login and registration form (not for public use, limited access).
- Two-level access: Standard user and administrator, where standard users have limited functionality.
- Logout button and automatic logout after longer absence.
- The search feature.

- Built-in function to review and select one or multiple selection of results with an option to save each search result.
- Function for optimal HTML code recognition and retrieval.
- Option for editing and storing results.

The search is carried out after we determine search criteria and constraints:

- Search within web pages or databases: User can select among default set of web pages, can define a new set of web pages, or can search over all pages on the web.
- Sort by popularity or time of publishing.
- Timeframe: There are three possibilities, the first is general search without specifying a timeframe, the second is entering the timeframe manually via the keyboard, and the last is clicking and selecting the timeframe within a built-in calendar.
- Search string: User can enter a keyword, a set of keywords, or other specified string for the proposed search.
- Minimal number of characters: We determine the length of a string in which the search string should appear.

An HTML code retriever enables the automatic recognition of HTML code. For this purpose we developed a universal text parser for all websites, and customized text parsers for the default set of web pages to enhance the acquisition of the content.

The metadata writer extract from a web page for further processing many elements, such as URL address, date and time, author, and keywords, and takes a screenshot of the web page.

The importance generator determines the importance of the content based on traffic ranks. We used two ranks: global rank (GR) and local rank (LR) (Alexa, Web). Global rank is an estimation of the site's popularity, and local rank is an estimation of the site's popularity in a specific country. Both ranks are calculated using a combination of average daily site visitors and page views over the past month. The site with the highest combination of visitors and page views is ranked the highest.

The marking of the search string and the screenshot of the site were accomplished using PhantomJS. We were able to access and manipulate DOM objects within web pages. Since PhantomJS uses WebKit, a real layout and rendering engine, it can capture a web page as a screenshot. PhantomJS can render anything on the web page so it can be used to convert contents not only in HTML and CSS, but also in SVG and Canvas (PhantomJS – Screen Capture, Web).

2.2 Databases

We used an open-source relational database management system (MySQL) to store information about search results such as article ID, the date of entry into the database, the URL of the parent web page, the URL of the news or article and its title and keywords, the name of the user who initiates the search, the importance of the web page (TR and GL rank), and a screenshot. For this reason we created 6 relational databases:

- Articles: current, archived, and deleted articles.
- Web pages: current and deleted web pages.
- Search strings.
- Sentiment: segmentation by document, paragraph and sentence.
- Users.
- Settings.

In relation to databases, the web application provides:

- An option to edit, archive and delete content.
- An option (built-in button) to retrieve and edit the entire HTML source code.
- Advanced search within databases, covering standard search, search by categories, transparent tabular view, selection of the number of shown objects, sorting according to the data of search results, etc.
- The option of exporting a report (generated as a pdf) that includes important information about the search results, including search settings, the web pages in which the content of the search results appeared, screenshots with marked search string, and a graphical display of results.

2.3 Sentiment Analysis

This component is part of another piece of research and is still under construction. In this research we retrieved 198,186 textual documents from five different Slovenian websites (www.24ur.com, www.dnevnik.si, www.

finance.si, www.rtvslo.si, and www.zurnal.si) enriched with political, business, economic, and finance content between September 1st 2007 and December 31st 2013. By labelling a sample of 10,500 documents we will obtain a labelled corpus; 6,500 documents have been labelled so far. These documents will be used as a training set to train, test, and evaluate classification techniques. The labelled corpus will also be publicly available for further research.

From the corpus of analysed unstructured data retrieved from the web, the following sentiment analysis will be performed:

- Filtering, cleaning, and pre-processing of data.
- Manual annotation of randomly selected textual content based on a five-level Likert scale (Likert 1932), where: 1 – very negative, 2 – negative, 3 – neutral, 4 – positive and 5 – very positive. To evaluate the process of annotation inter-rater and intra-rater reliability will be used.
- Tokenization, transcription, stop words, stemming, and lemmatization will be tried (Lemmatise, Web). With tokenization we break a textual stream into words, phrases, or other meaningful tokens. In the process of transcription we optionally convert letters to lower case, remove numbers, etc. Often it is also useful to remove some of the most common words (stop words). Stemming is a frequently used process to reduce words and unify various forms of words to their root form (stem), while lemmatization groups different words so that they can be analysed as a single item (lemma).
- Testing and integration of machine learning algorithms for the classification of sentiment; performance and evaluation of tested classification algorithms.
- Branding of the company (identification sentiment about the company, evaluating response to posts and analysis).

3 Challenges

Due to the complexity of the project we had some issues, which we managed to overcome successfully. However, there were challenges with the implementation of our solutions in the Google Custom Search Engine, such as integration of search within timeframe, adding an option to select and store each search result, adaptation of software code due to occasional modifications of the engine's scripts, and compromises regarding the desired solutions and the limitations of supporting environments.

We also encountered some difficulties when we retrieved the textual contents from HTML code. Apparently, web pages do vary widely. It was necessary to develop customized text parsers to enhance the acquisition of the content. We realized that many web pages contain errors in the HTML code which cause some difficulties in obtaining web content efficiently, so it was necessary to develop a solution that supports the option of manual input or editing by the user.

One of the greatest challenges was how to generate screenshots and store them into the database. The screenshots we obtained show the real content of web pages in high resolution, which takes up a lot of space. There were some issues in finding the optimal format which takes up minimal space and yet still supports satisfactory resolution.

In addition, we also had some difficulties confronting hackers' attacks on our server; these limited the functionality of our web application. Over time, we improved security solutions so all scripts on the server ran smoothly. All of the challenges we experienced were constantly under prudent and rational consideration and we found concrete solutions to them.

4 Challenges

In this paper we briefly introduced the results of a web clipping project. The project was focused on the development of a web solution for selecting, retrieving, extracting, and tracking information in publicly available publications on the web.

New technologies and open access to an enormous amount of online data generate new ideas for future innovations. However, humankind is still hungry for knowledge derived from retrieved information. Knowledge is the engine of progress. For many reasons, it is absolutely impossible to employ readers to obtain important information about customers, competitors, or company operations, organization, marketing, sales, engineering, and product and service quality. With the use of appropriate technology and knowledge we can overcome these challenges.

We live in the information age, where the right information at the right time and the right place is crucial for success. An organization that has control over information can quickly respond to market trends and improve strategic decisions in the future.

While the system we have described is still under development, the results so far are encouraging. Users appreciate implemented solutions. The web module is based and designed on research studies, user feedback, and implemented solutions, which will be improved and upgraded. We plan to simultaneously enhance the automation of processes; thus the project will not become obsolete. Similar solutions are highly sought after and respected; therefore they evolve rapidly.

Acknowledgments

Work supported by Creative Core FISNM-3330-13-500033 'Simulations' project funded by the European Union, The European Regional Development Fund and Nevtron & Company d.o.o. research voucher founded by the Ministry of Education, Science and Sport, Slovenia. The operation is carried out within the framework of the Operational Programme for Strengthening Regional Development Potentials for the period 2007–2013, Development Priority 1: Competitiveness and Research Excellence, Priority Guideline 1.1: Improving the Competitive Skills and Research Excellence.

References

Alexa, retrieved 24.4.2014, from http://www.alexa.com/.

Breiman, Leo, et al.: *Classification and* Regression *Trees.* Wadsworth & Brooks/Cole Advanced Books & Software, Monterey, California, USA 1984, pp. 18–55.

Cortes, Corinna / Vapnik, Vladimir: "Support Vector Networks." *Machine Learning* 20(3), 1995, pp. 273–297.

Cover, Thomas / Hart, Peter: "Nearest Neighbour Pattern Classification." *IEEE Transactions on Information Theory* 13(1), 1967, pp. 21–27.

Gomes, Pedro, et. al.: "Web Clipping: Compression Heuristics for Displaying Text on a PDA." *Mobile HCI'01*, 2001, pp. 1–6.

Google Alerts, retrieved 5.5.2014, from http://www.google.com/alerts.

Google Custom Search Engine, retrieved 15.4.2014, from https://www.google.com/cse/.

Harrell, Frank. E.: *Regression Modeling Strategies.* Springer-Verlag, New York, USA 2001, pp. 11–37.

Haykin, Simon: *Neural Networks: A Comprehensive Foundation.* Macmillan, New York, USA 1994, pp. 1–45.

Lemmatise, retrieved 20.5.2014, from http://lemmatise.ijs.si/Software/.

Lewis, David D.: "Naïve (Bayes) at Forty: The Independent Assumption in Information Retrieval." *Proceedings of a 10th European Conference on Machine Learning*, 1998, pp. 4–15.

Likert, Rensis: *A Technique for the Measurement of Attitudes.* Archives of Psychology, New York, USA 1932, pp. 1–55.

Liu, Bing: "Sentiment Analysis and Subjectivity." In N. Indurkhya and F. J. Damerau (eds), *Handbook of Natural Language Processing* 2nd edn., 2010, pp. 627–666.

Michalski, Ryszard S.: "Discovering Classification Rules Using Variable-Valued Logic System VL." *Proceedings of a Third International Joint Conference on Artificial Intelligence*, Stanford, California, USA 1973, pp. 62–172.

PhantomJS – Screen Capture, retrieved 26.4.2014, from http://phantomjs. org/screen-capture.html.

Računalniške novice, retrieved 10.4.2014, from http://www.racunalniske-novice.com.

Sanger, J. / Feldman, R.: *The Text Mining Handbook.* Cambridge Univ. Press, New York, 2007, pp. 94–129.

Web Clipping, retrieved 10.4.2014, from http://www.webclipping.com.

Andrej Kovačič
Faculty for Media, Ljubljana, Slovenia,
Nevenka Podgornik
School of Advanced Social Studies in Nova Gorica, Slovenia

Sharing Personal Information on the Internet Empowers Relationship Marketing

Abstract: The internet seems to bring incredible advantages for marketers, in terms of reducing costs, expanding time horizons, and increasing their organization's reach. We aim to present personal information-sharing on the internet as the enabling factor for the future development of relationship marketing. Our study has in this respect provided evidence that the majority (especially of younger consumers) are prepared to provide the required personal information in order to receive a more personalised service. Thus, despite enormous privacy concerns over relationship marketing, there seems to be majority compliance with the new internet environment.

Keywords: internet, communication, relationship marketing

1 Introduction

Relationship marketing can be defined, according to Kotler (1997), as the practice of building long-term satisfying relations with key parties – customers, suppliers, distributors – in order to retain their long-term preference and business. The principal aim of relationship marketing is thus to build, develop, and maintain the relationship with the customer as an individual, rather than target an anonymous mass broken up into homogenous segments. This approach is, according to Cova (1999), justified by the following arguments:

- If the market can no longer be cut up into stable segments, the only alternative is to address the consumer individually.
- If consumers are unpredictable, it is not as important to predict their behavior as it is to be able to react immediately to their aspirations through the maintenance of a continuous relationship.

- If consumers wish to differentiate themselves, they ask for personalized products and services, which only a continuous, close relationship can assure.

Although these arguments may be new, the concept of relationship marketing is not. Different marketing techniques have long been tested to establish a personalized and individual relationship with the customer. Nevertheless, it is with new information and communication technologies used on the internet that some relationship marketing strategies have become affordable and economically acceptable (for example with Facebook). Targeting consumers as individuals, however, requires that consumers share their personal information to provide marketers with sufficient data for personalization. In market share statistics (Web Cross-Channel Marketing Report 2013) based on a 2013 survey of nearly 900 companies, just 22 % of companies were conducting no relationship marketing at all, whereas 30 % companies said they were "very committed" to relationship marketing and 46 % were committed to a certain extent.

2 Change in Value for Consumers

Besides enabling some new marketing strategies, the new environment has completely changed the way companies communicate and deliver value to their customers. On the internet the burden is on marketers to animate consumers who are now actively involved in their own message construction. Active involvement, however, often comes at the cost of sacrificing their privacy. In fact many marketers are saying that this phenomenon is changing the whole field of marketing in fundamental ways.

The first factor which affects the building of a relationship with consumers is technology. The internet, for example, makes certain strategies affordable and expands the capacity for relationship marketing. As Sisodia and Wolfe (2000) argue, there is a „symbiotic relationship between technology advances and the change in marketing paradigm toward relationship marketing." This cycle can clearly be seen in Figure 1.

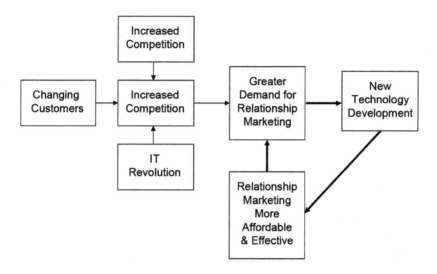

Fig 1: A cycle between IT and relationship marketing
Source: Sisodia and Wolfe (2000)

The greater demand for relationship marketing has triggered the development of new technology. With new technology, relationship marketing becomes more affordable and effective. Figure 1 also shows us that the incentive for relationship marketing comes in part from developments in informational technology, from rising customer expectation, greater competitive pressures, and changes in marketing thinking.

The second driver towards relationship marketing is a change in customer behavior. Some marketing principles may never change, for example customers trust good brands and companies. Nevertheless, as the internet gains in importance and companies lose their market share, many marketers want to understand which of their repeatedly-tested concepts might need modification. Yet relationship marketers are limited by the "willingness" of consumers to share their personal information on the internet. If privacy concerns prevail, relationship marketers can find themselves trapped by insufficient and falsified information and requests.

The internet is not like other media and it is only by understanding its characteristics that marketers may extend their internet marketing benefits to their full capacity. In the new environment marketers have to learn new

„rules of the market" to be able to implement (sometimes radical) necessary changes towards relationship marketing. By understanding the new environment marketers may at the same time discover that many of these „rules" speak in favor of (and may to some extent justify) a relationship marketing approach.

3 New „Rules" for Marketers

With the informational age marketers face changes in consumer markets. The "new rules" can be summarized by the following points. First, the internet has become a collection of niche communities. Despite millions of users, the internet must not be understood as a mass medium. Second, there is a power shift from a "passive audience" to online consumers who actively select which internet content they are interested in. They decide what marketing information they will receive, about which products and services, and under what conditions. In online marketing, the consumer, with a control of the mouse, controls the interaction. Third, markets face increased velocity in delivering value to their customers and in changing the environment. Everyone, including competitors, knows instantly what the other is doing. Fourth, knowledge management becomes vital. As Strauss, Frost and El-Ansary (2008) stress, the technology automatically records the actions of users in a digital format that can be easily, quickly, and mathematically calculated and analyzed. Marketing managers can track the results of their strategies as they are implemented.

Organizations build large databases of information, often neglecting privacy considerations. This information can then be turned into marketing knowledge and can provide a strong tool for implementing relationship marketing strategies. Finally, as Strauss et al. (2008) argue, there is now a shift towards a new matrix organizational structure and thus towards a new interdisciplinary approach in marketing. Marketing departments can no longer develop and implement strategies alone. Social sciences and consumer psychology play an increasingly important role in understanding the true nature of the relationship between consumers and companies.

4 Forming a Relationship – More Sales with Existing Consumers

A company's demand can derive from new customers and repeat customers. Traditional marketing theory and practice have focused on attracting new customers while little was done to keep them. This preoccupation with customer acquisition rather than customer retention has been criticized as a ‚leaky bucket' approach to business (Payne 2000). As long as enough new customers are acquired to replace those existing customers lost through the hole in the bucket, success in the form of sales is achieved. Mudie (1997) estimated that most organizations lose significantly more than 30 per cent of their customers before or at the time of a repurchase decision, mainly through poor service and neglecting the collaboration. In the past growing markets meant a sufficient supply of new customers. Companies could, according to Mudie (1997), keep filling the marketing bucket with new customers without worrying about losing old customers through holes in the bottom of the bucket.

Today, however, as Kotler and Armstrong (1997) argue, companies are facing some new marketing realities and the emphasis is shifting. Among these are changing demographics, a slow-growth economy, competitors that are more sophisticated, over-production capacity and fewer new customers. Consequently the costs of attracting new customers are rising and now, according to Kotler and Armstrong (1997), it costs five times as much to attract a new customer than to keep the current ones. Additionally, companies are realizing that losing a customer means not only losing a single sale but losing the entire stream of purchases that a certain customer does in a lifetime.

Finally, the problem of traditional transaction marketing production is that the increasingly turbulent and fragmented market demands a greater and greater variety of goods and services. Transaction marketers focusing on sale tend to respond to these needs by developing more and more products. However, at the end, as Payne (2000) argues, "companies only bombard their customers with too many choices from which the customers cannot find the right one for their individual needs – customers do not want more choices. They want exactly when, what, where, and how they want it." Technology can be combined with a relationship marketing knowledge to help companies deliver better services and products. First, interactive database technology enables companies to gather large amounts of data on an individual customer's needs and preferences. Second, information technology and flexible manufacturing systems enable companies to customize large volumes of goods or services for individual customers at a relatively low cost (Peppers, Rogers & Dorf 2000). Apart from designing strategies to attract new customers and create transactions with them, companies are now practicing relationship marketing. The emphasis is on maintaining profitable long-term relationships with customers by creating superior customer value and satisfaction. The shift towards relationship marketing thinking can be seen in Figure 2.

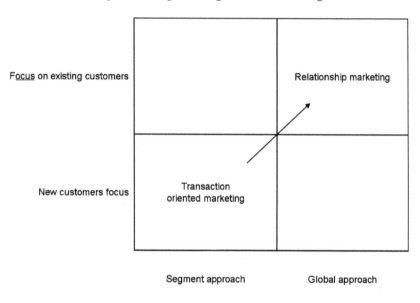

Fig. 2: The shift towards relationship marketing

The relationship concept at first appeared to be suitable only for a niche market of rich clients. Today, modern IT, and particularly the new interactive medium of the internet, provides an opportunity to bring personalized and customized products to the mass market at a mass-produced price. Nevertheless, this concept requires new thinking that breaks away from the traditional concepts of transaction-oriented mass marketing and mass production. The most important differences are summarized in Table 1.

Table 1: The differences between transactional and relationship marketing

Transactional paradigm concept	Relationship paradigm concept	Comments
Market segment	Individual customer	Transactional marketing identifies a statistical customer – the hypothetical human who is composed of statistically averaged attributes drawn from research. Relationship marketing focuses on individual customer needs.
Duration of transaction	Lifetime relationship	The pursuit of customer loyalty is more of a journey.
Margin	Lifetime	The justification of a relationship approach is the lifetime value of these prospective customers, not the unit sale.
Market share	Most valued customers	For companies implementing relationship marketing, relationships with the customers are more important than the current and unstable market share.
Mass marketing monologue	Direct marketing	The new marketing requires feedback as a two-way communication.
Passive consumers	Empowered clients	Transactional marketing is all about seduction and propaganda and it depends on a passive, narcotized receptor – the legendary "couch potato".

Source: Adapted from Chaffey, Mayer & Johnston. (2000)

Despite the apparently clear separation, many companies find themselves somewhere between the transactional and relationship concept (Rapp & Giehler, 1999). This is happening mainly because companies are often reluctant to change quickly and radically especially in this early stage of relationship marketing adoption where everyone is testing new concepts and waiting for results. In the future, however, wider gaps between companies implementing and those not implementing relationship marketing are expected. In addition to a company's intention to implement relationship marketing, success will also be measured by the global (as well as the company's) ability to persuade consumers to share their personal information. This is especially important in the introduction of relationship marketing as consumers still determine the real value of customised products and services.

5. Research Work

We have conducted a short piece of quantitative field research to determine whether younger generations of consumers are keener on relationship marketing than older generations (and so allow more personal information to be shared and used by marketers).

The purpose of this study was thus to assess people's abilities to protect personal data on the internet and the level to which these rights are exercised. We aimed to prove that new generations of young consumers have a more flexible approach to privacy concerns, enabling further developments in relationship marketing. The following hypotheses were formed in this respect:

H1: The self-reflected knowledge about computers to protect personal data is higher for younger consumers.

H2: Fewer younger consumers exercise the power they have to protect their data than older consumers.

H3: A greater number of younger consumers publish self-made content (photos, videos, information about their work or about what they are doing, or other personal current info) than older consumers.

H4: A greater number of younger consumers have profiles on social networks.

The sample of the Slovenian population included a total of 318 respondents. Field work was conducted in three locations: Ljubljana, Nova Gorica and Novo mesto. The interviewing was combined with a longer questionnaire (15 min) to reduce overall costs. Due to errors only 301 were included in the analysis, setting the confidence interval at 4.52. The research was conducted in a controlled environment in 235 cases. In 66 cases the questionnaire was filled out in the absence of a researcher (the online method). The respondents' average income was also within the national income average. The data was analyzed using SPSS PASW Statistics 18 software. A little more than a half of the respondents were sampled within a younger consumers group (18–24 years) to enable a good comparison analysis.

Table 2: Sample to population age group comparison

Age group in years	Population in %	Sample in %
15–24	11.8	51.2
25–64	67.6	34.2
65 +	20.2	13.0
Sum	100	100

6. Results

For H1 we tested whether the younger respondents evaluated their knowledge to protect their personal data differently than other age groups. To answer the hypothesis we used the chi-square test that is most often used with nominal data, where observations are grouped into several discrete, mutually exclusive categories. As data are assumed to be a random sample, independence between each observation recorded in each category was achieved. Each subject had only one entry in the chi-square table. The expected frequency for each category for all tests was more than 5.

From the chi-square test we can see that the chi-square value is significant, chi-square(df = 2) = 16.48 p < 0.01. There is a significant difference in the population about self-reported knowledge to protect personal data on the internet. It seems that 92.5 % of younger consumers (below 25) believe that is true, compare to 73.3 % of 25–64 years old and to 60.0 % of those above 65. Thus we can confirm the H1 that a greater number of younger consumers believe that they are able to protect their personal data on the internet.

Having proven the ability to protect their personal data, H2 aims to answer whether or not this ability is exercised more often by younger consumers. We found out that fewer (82.6 %) younger consumers (those below 25) have done something to protect their personal data than those in the 25–64 age group, where 86.8 % had done so. However the chi-square test did not show significant differences and H2 could not be confirmed.

Testing H3 we found out that substantially more (83.7 %) younger consumers published self-created content on the internet compared to 55.9 %

of those aged 25–64 and to 42.3 % of those aged above 65. This difference is significant at p < 0.01 with chi-square(df = 2) = 16.48. We can accept H3, that more younger consumers publish self-made content (photos, videos, information about their work or about what they are doing or other personal current information) than any other age group.

Finally we can accept H4 as 96.6 % of younger consumers have a social network profile compared to 66.5 % of 25–64 year olds, and 50.0 % of those above 65 years old. The difference is statistically significant: chi-square(df = 2) = 36.91 at p< 0.01 level.

7. Interpretation and Further Research

This study, the tables for which are presented in the appendix, confirmed academic hunches about the behaviours surrounding the sharing of personal data on the internet. Thus we found evidence which shows that on average consumers are more than willing to share their personal information on the internet and that, by doing so, marketers can get sufficient and reliable data to set up relationship marketing. Our study also offers evidence that simply because we are able to share our data with the unknown service provider we are indeed entering a global relationship marketing period on the internet. Yet, despite the fact that this study may suggest the trend of future development, it cannot promise that this trend is irreversible. This makes relationship marketing a promising area of research that deserves greater consideration. Further research should also be conducted in other demographic, educational, geographical, and cultural contexts as well as by varying the media-related characteristics. At the same time, additional instruments should be developed to analyse the implementation and development of relationship marketing in the future. In addition to the self-reporting scale employed in this study, qualitative research should also be carried out in future studies.

8. Conclusion

The basic idea of relationship marketing is to focus mainly on keeping existing customers. It seems that the parallelism between the forces of technological change and radically new thinking in marketing has been highly fortuitous. The internet has emerged just in time to allow marketers to implement many essential aspects of relationship marketing. The new technologies have become more affordable, enabling marketers to deploy them more widely. The nature of the internet, as a collection of niche communities, and new rules, such as power shift, increased velocity, the importance of knowledge management, and the interdisciplinary focus, can all be seen as reasons for applying relationship marketing on the internet. To what extent relationship marketing can be applied to other markets (suppliers, referral, internal, influence, and recruitment) remains to be seen. In addition cross-influences between what the markets are, and what additional benefits can be expected when relationship marketing is applied to every aspect of a company, have yet to be investigated.

Understanding the internet and those relationships that can be sustained over a long period are undoubtedly vitally important for marketers implementing strategies in the future. The internet clearly empowers relationship marketing. The two forces are empowering one another and therefore instead of addressing them separately we need to focus on a combined sociological, as well as economical, approach.

On the other hand, implementing technology is not enough by itself. Consumers must to some extent be willing to share their personal information. As it seems that marketers have to a large extent succeeded in convincing younger consumers, especially, that sharing is the "way" on the internet, we may be seeing an exponential increase in relationship marketing. As the majority of consumers tend to accept these new rules there might be no other alternative for non-conformers who still want to preserve their right to privacy. Thus the internet will be making the relationship between the marketer and consumer increasingly more personalized whether consumers or companies like this change or not. This may enable a greater potential for one-to-one relationship marketing, a new relationship marketing paradigm. It will bring companies and customers even closer together, enabling them to learn even more from each other.

A vital role in relationship marketing presents information about the individual consumer's needs. Here the willingness of consumers to share their personal information is essential. The study we have presented has shown that consumers (especially those in the younger generations) are willing to open the door for this information to be (ab)used in a relationship marketing context. The next step toward mass customization may thus be closer than we tend to believe. Information has to be turned into marketing knowledge used for mass customization so that companies can deliver products or services tailored to the individual's needs, and thus increase value for consumers. If marketers succeed sufficiently in creating new values that prevail over concerns about privacy we shall be facing a global relationship marketing expansion.

References

Chaffey, Dave / Mayer, Richard / Johnston, Kevin: "Internet Marketing: Strategy, Implementation and Practice." Harlow: Pearson Education Ltd., 2000.

Cova, Bernard: „From Marketing to Societing: "When the Link Is More Important than the Thing." In Douglas Brownlie, Mike Saren, Robin Wensley et al. (eds), *Rethinking Marketing: Towards Critical Marketing Accountings*. SAGE Publications: London, Califomia, 1999, pp. 64–84.

Kotler, Philip: *Marketing Management: Analysis, Planning, Implementation and Control*, 8th edn. New Jersey: Prentice Hall International, Inc., 1997.

Kotler, Philip / Armstrong, Gary: *Marketing: An Introduction*, 4th edn. New, Jersey: Prentice-Hall International, Inc., 1997.

Mudie, Peter: *Marketing: An Analytical Perspective*. London: Prentice Hall Europe, 1997.

Payne, Adrian: "Relationship Marketing: The UK Perspective." In Jagdish N. Sheth & Atul Parvatiyar (eds), *Handbook of Relationship Marketing*. Sage Publications Inc.: Thousand Oaks, 2000, pp. 39–69.

Peppers, Don / Rogers, Martha / Dorf, Bob: "Do You Want to Keep Your Customers Forever?" In James H. Gilmore & Joseph B. Pine II (eds): *Markets of One, Creating Customer-Unique Value through Mass Customization*. Harvard Business Review Books, 2000, pp. 75–99.

Rapp, Reinhold / Giehler, Miriam: "Relationship Marketing im Intemet." In Adrian Payne & Reinhold Rapp (eds): *Handbuch Relationship Marketing: Konzeption und erfolgreiche Unsetzung*. München Verlag Franz Vahlen GmbH, 1999, pp. 275–291.

Sisodia, Rajendra S. / Wolfe, David B.: "Informational Technology: Its Role in Building, Maintaining and Enhancing Relations." In Jagdish N. Sheth

& Atul Parvatiyar (eds): *Handbook of Relationship Marketing*. Sage Publications Inc.: Thousand Oaks, 2000, pp. 525–556.

Strauss, Judy / Frost, Raymond / El-Ansary, Adel: *E-Marketing*, 8th edn. New Jersey: Prentice Hall International, Inc., 2008.

Web Cross-Channel Marketing Report, retrieved 5.5.2014 from http://econsultancy.com/si/reports/cross-channel-marketing-report, 2013.

Appendix

Table A1: Is your knowledge sufficient to protect your personal data? * Age group cross-tabulation

Is your knowledge sufficient to protect your personal data?		Age group			Total
		less than 25	25–64	above 65	
yes	Count	74	121	15	210
	% within Age group	92,5 %	73,3 %	60,0 %	77,8 %
no	Count	6	44	10	60
	% within Age group	7,5 %	26,7 %	40,0 %	22,2 %
Total	Count	80	165	25	270
	% within Age group	100,0 %	100,0 %	100,0 %	100,0 %

Table A4: Do you have a social network profile? * Age group cross-tabulation

Do you have a social network profile?		Age group			Total
		less than 25	25–64	above 65	
yes	Count	85	123	14	222
	% within Age group	96,6 %	66,5 %	50,0 %	73,8 %
no	Count	3	62	14	79
	% within Age group	3,4 %	33,5 %	50,0 %	26,2 %
Total	Count	88	185	28	301
	% within Age group	100,0 %	100,0 %	100,0 %	100,0 %

Gregor Polančič and Boštjan Orban
Faculty of Electrical Engineering and Computer Science, University of Maribor

An Extension of BPMN 2.0 Conversation Diagrams for Modeling Organizational Communication

Abstract: Business Process Model and Notation (BPMN) is process modeling standard which can be used in almost any business domain. With the release of BPMN 2.0, a new subtype of diagrams was introduced – conversation diagrams. They are primarily used for modeling 'process landscapes' as well as basic interactions between different process participants. However, since the notation is simple and extendable, our primary objective was to investigate if the notation could be applicable for modeling organizational communication, if necessary by extending it with additional elements for that purpose. By considering conversation diagrams and similar diagraming techniques (e.g. UML, ARIS and EPC), we defined 15 new elements on three different abstract levels – conceptual, logical and physical, and implemented extended elements into three diagraming tools.

Keywords: BPMN 2.0, conversation diagrams, conversation node, organizational communication, e-communication, push technologies

1 Introduction

Business Process Model and Notation (BPMN) is an ISO standardized graphical notation for modeling business processes. The first version of BPMN was introduced in 2005. In 2009, the Object Management Group (OMG) prepared a draft for the second BPMN version, which introduced the idea of modeling conversations. The final release of BPMN 2.0 was published in January 2011 and included notations and models for representing business processes, collaborations, choreographies and conversations (Chinosi & Trombetta 2012). Conversation diagrams (hereinafter referred to as CD) are used to represent high-level interactions between involved parties (Allweyer 2010). They are useful for representing an overview of a network of partners and how they communicate with each other. A weakness of CD is lack of elements which could present different types of organizational communication processes in details, including e-communication (Chinosi & Trombetta 2012). In this paper, we introduce the idea of extending CD with new intuitive and understandable elements which are suited for the modeling and representation of communication processes in organizational settings – organizational communication (Allweyer 2010, OMG 2011).

Organizational communication is defined as the process by which individuals stimulate meaning in the minds of other individuals by means of verbal and nonverbal messages in the context of a formal organization (Richmond & McCroskey 2008). Communication serves six functions in organizations, which are informing, regulating, integrating, managing, persuading and socializing. Informing is a function of providing required information to stakeholders so they can perform their job. The regulative function is involved with the communication that is directed toward regulatory policies within the organization or messages about maintenance in organization. Integration is important when communication is focused to achieve a common goal with coordination of tasks, work assignments and group coordination. The management function is important when communication is focused on getting employees to perform required tasks, learning information about them and establishing relationships with stakeholders. The persuasive function is an outgrowth of the management function. The last function is socializing, which is often neglected but which is perhaps the most important one, since it determines whether individuals are being integrated into the communication network of an organization (Turkalj & Fosic 2009).

2 BPMN 2.0 Conversation Diagrams

BPMN 2.0 conversation diagrams (CD) notation consists of seven visual elements. Two elements represent different participants whereas four elements are conversation node elements. The last notation element is a connection line between a participant and a conversation. The participant is visualized as a BPMN pool and represents people, organizations or devices which are involved in a certain communication. The second participant element is 'multiple participant', which is recognized by the symbol "|||" (Figure 1), and represents several equal instances of participants. The other four elements are conversation node elements, which are graphically represented as hexagons. The basic conversation node element is conversation, which defines communication between two or more participants (Figure 1). Semantically, a conversation element can be expanded into a series of message flows between participants. In cases where a conversation element has the symbol "+", it represents a sub-conversation which can be expanded into a series of message flows as well as conversations. It is similar to a sub-process in a business process diagram (Allweyer 2010, OMG 2011).

Global conversation and collaboration elements are represented as hexagons with thick borders (Figure 1). Their aim is to reuse and integrate with other diagrams. Global conversation reuses the attributes and properties of other instances of diagrams, whereas the collaboration element can be called upon by other collaboration diagrams (OMG 2011, Shapiro et al. 2011).

The conversation link connects conversation node elements with participants. It is graphically represented with a solid double line (Figure 1). The conversation link always connects conversation node elements with participants, where it is not allowed to connect two same types of elements (Shapiro et al. 2011).

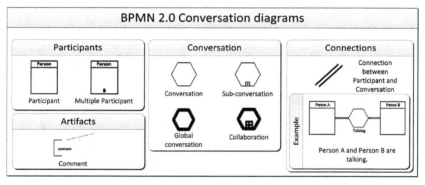

Fig. 1: BPMN 2.0 conversation diagrams notation

We performed a SWOT analysis of the strengths, weaknesses, opportunities and threats of conversation diagram, which is presented in Table 1.

Table 1: SWOT matrix for conversation diagrams

Strengths	Weaknesses
• Presentation of a process-landscape view. • Quickly learnable elements and rules (Chinosi & Trombetta 2012) • Unique shapes for elements (Chinosi & Trombetta 2011).	• Lack of elements for modeling organizational processes (Chinosi & Trombetta 2012). • No elements to present e-communication in organizational processes. • Inability to determine the type of participant.
Opportunities	Threats
• Could be useful for organizations where communication is important. • Has potential for standalone use (communication view). • Could be extended with additional elements and concepts.	• Lack of elements for real-world communication could decrease acceptance. • Conversation diagrams could stay in the shadow of successful business process diagrams.

As evident from Table 1, CD are quickly learnable and easy to understand to new and existing users. This probably results from the fact that they consists of a small number of unique symbols. On the other hand, it is sometimes difficult to model the complex communications which appears in real organizational settings, including e-communication; this highlights an opportunity to extend the notation to make it more applicable and useful.

3 Proposed Solution

The main objective of extending CD was to define additional elements to represent organizational communications such as e-communication and SOA (Service-Oriented Architecture), which was perceived as a weakness in related studies (Allweyer 2010). Since representing complex organizational communication might detrimentally affect the simplicity of a diagram, we proposed a three-level (conceptual, logical and physical level) modeling approach, which has already proved successful in the field of database modeling.

3.1 Review of Related Fields

In order to assure the ease of use and usefulness of the proposed extensions of CD (hereinafter referred to as extended Conversation diagrams – xCD), we searched for similar ideas in other notations and related fields, such as UML, ARIS EPC and the theory of databases. We also incorporated the recommendations for designing new graphical notations proposed by Larkin and Simon (1987). Nine recommendations for the successful design of a new notation were identified: semiotic clarity, perceptual discriminability, semantic transparency, complexity management, cognitive integration, visual expressiveness, dual coding, graphic economy and cognitive fit (Larkin & Simon 1987). Additionally, the graphical symbols should also satisfy the requirements of the construction of new elements (redundancy, overload, excess and deficit) (Larkin & Simon 1987, Moody 2009). Regarding the modeling notations, our proposal incorporates several ideas from Unified Modeling Language (UML), a language for data, business and object modeling (Eloranta, Kallio & Terho 2006; Rumbaugh, Jacobson & Booch 2004). It has 12 different diagrams, which are most commonly used in software engineering. In case of UML, we reused the idea of connecting related elements, like generalizations and extensions in UML Use case diagrams, which was added to xCD. We also analyzed UML Sequence diagrams, where we identified some ideas for new elements. One of ideas, which was taken from Sequence diagrams, was how to define the type of participant. We identified three different types of participants: a device, a person and an organization (Figure 2). Another idea, which was obtained from Sequence diagrams was the concept of a sequence flow – an idea to keep the same order of messages in each instance of a conversation.

Yet another set of ideas was obtained from an Event-driven Process Chain (EPC), which is part of Architecture of Integrated Information Systems (ARIS). EPC is useful for modeling, analyzing and reengineering business processes. It is also easy for modeling and has a good semantic to describe business processes (Dumas, van der Aalst & ter Hofstede 2005). EPC's element 'process path' has been adapted to xCD's navigation element 'background conversation' (Figure 2). By using this element, we can model detailed conversation on a separate model.

Several ideas were also obtained from other parts of BPMN (i.e. process diagrams and collaboration diagrams); for example, we decided to reuse the artifacts (comments), annotation of rules, navigation, events and the idea of complex conversation between participants (Figure 2). One of the main objectives for extending CD was to support e-communication. For this purpose, we reused the concepts of Service-Oriented architecture (SOA) message exchange methods – the one way, two way and data stream concept (Erl 2005).

In the theory of databases we found the idea how to present new elements in a way that they will be understandable for users and computers. In the development of database modeling it is common to define the models on three levels. This follows from Popper's three worlds, named as World 1, World 2 and World 3 (Popper 1978). The conceptual level (World 1) is suitable for users and represents symbols of the real world. The logical (World 2) level is intended for advanced users and also for computer recognition. The physical level (World 3) is mostly suitable for computers (Husemann, Lechtenbörger & Vossen 2000).

3.2 Extended conversation diagrams

After considering related fields and our SWOT analysis of CD, we defined 15 new elements (Figure 2).

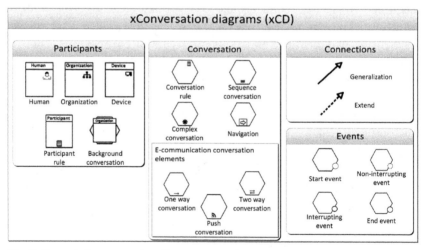

Fig. 2: Extended conversation diagrams notation

Table 2 summarizes new elements, together with their descriptions, examples and primary notation.

Table 2: New elements and connections

Element name	Description	Examples	Primary notation
Participant – Person	Type of participant is a person or group of people.	Participant in conversation is an engineer, a doctor, etc.	UML Use case, BPMN
Participant – Organization	Type of participant is an organization.	Participant in conversation is a computer, a company, a bank, etc.	UML Use case, EPC.
Participant – Device	Type of participant is a device.	Participant in conversation is a computer, a smart phone, etc.	UML Use case, BPMN
Participant rule	Participants must comply with the defined rules, written in a comment.	Participant 'Engineer' must have a Java license.	BPMN
Background conversation	Navigation element that points to the separate model of organization conversation.	We are interested in the communication within the company. So, we present organization conversation on a separate model.	EPC
Conversation rule	Conversation must comply with the defined rules, written in a comment.	Conversation takes places in the CEO's office.	BPMN
Complex conversation	Conversation between three or more participants, where details of conversation are not important.	Supplier, dealer and company have complex conversation.	BPMN

Element name	Description	Examples	Primary notation
Navigation	Navigation elements that points to the separate model of a conversation.	Conversation is too complex to be modeled on the same model.	BPMN
Sequence conversation	Specifies the order of message flows.	Order of messages when asking for a credit is same in any case.	UML Sequence diagram, BPMN 2.0
One way conversation	Same direction of messages.	Weather sensor is sending data to the server.	SOA
Two way conversation	Every message is in different direction than the last one.	Servers are exchanging processed data.	SOA
Push conversation	The first and the last message is in the same direction, where the remaining messages' directions are reversed.	RSS, e-mail newsletters, live scores, etc.	SOA
Events	Events begin, terminate or end conversation.	E-mail, received from a bank, starts the conversation.	BPMN
Generalization	A participant inherits the rights from another participant.	CEO has the same rights as an engineer. Additionally he can arrange new business.	UML Use case
Extend	Optional possibility to start other Conversation elements.	Successful completion of negotiations can start a new conversation about new jobs.	UML Use case

As evident from Table 2, the proposed xCD notation extends CD notation in all aspects: participants, types of conversations and connections, where the majority of ideas for new elements were obtained from BPMN, UML and SOA. The next two subchapters present the details of two new elements – a new conversation node and a new connection.

3.3 An Example of an Extended Conversation Diagram Element – Push Conversation

A push conversation element was introduced since this type of conversation is common in SOA and e-communication. The element represents push technologies, like RSS, the live-score website concept, instant messaging, mail newsletters, etc. Since push conversation is commonly implemented with RSS technology, its visual representation was obtained from RSS (Figure 3).

Fig. 3: Push conversation element – graphical representation (conceptual level)

On the logical level, the push conversation element is represented with a series of message flows (Figure 4). In addition, it is important that the type of participants which are connected to push conversation are (must be) devices. In the case of a push conversation, the direction of messages between two devices is also important. The first and the last message go in the same direction, whereas the remaining messages' directions are reversed.

Fig. 4: Push conversation element element on logical level

The physical level of the push conversation element is readable for devices and is therefore defined in XML format. XML have to be consistent with the following XML Schema Definition (XSD) of the push conversation element.

```
<xsd:element name="pushConversation"
type="tConversationNode"/>
<xsd:complexType name="tConversationNode">
<xsd:complexContent>
        <xsd:extension base="tBaseElement">
            <xsd:sequence>
            <xsd:element name="messageFlowRef"
type="xsd:QName" minOccurs="0"
maxOccurs="unbounded"/>
            <xsd:element name="participantRef"
type="xsd:QName" minOccurs="0"
maxOccurs="unbounded" fixed="Device"/>
            <xsd:element name="boundaryEventRefs"
type="xsd:QName" minOccurs="0"
maxOccurs="1"/>
            </xsd:sequence>
            <xsd:attribute name="conversationRef"
type="xsd:QName"/>
            <xsd:attribute
name="correlationKeyRef"
type="xsd:QName"/>
            <xsd:attribute name="extendFlowRefs"
type="xsd:QName" use="optional"/>
            </xsd:extension>
        </xsd:complexContent>
</xsd:complexType>
```

The above XSD consists of references of message flows, participant, boundary, conversation, correlation key and extend flow, which is optional. References are links to XSD Schemas of BPMN standard and our newly build XSDs. Figure 5 represents an example of a push conversation element. The element must be connected with two or more devices (e.g. server and tablet computer). Other types of participants, like organization or person are not allowed to connect with a push conversation element. This element could present technologies like RSS, instant messaging, etc.

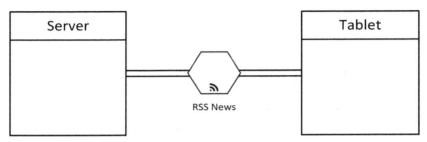

Fig. 5: Push conversation example

3.4 An Example of an Extended Conversation Diagram Connection – Generalization

CD contain only one connection between conversation elements – a pipeline. It is represented with a two straight lines connecting two or more conversation elements (Allweyer 2010). Based on the analysis of CD and organizational communication, we proposed two new connections – Generalization and Extend. These two connections are a primary part of UML (Use case diagrams and Class diagrams) and share the same meaning in xCD.

Connection Extend is useful when conversation has one or more additional conversations which might be optional in a conversation process. It is represented as a dashed line with arrow on the end of line. The other connection, we propose is Generalization, which connects two participants. It is represented as a solid line with a triangle on the end and means that one participant (the target of a generalization) in the conversation process will have additional rights to the other one (the source of generalization).

Fig. 6: Connection Generalization

The following example (Figure 7) represents two participants in a conversation – an IT worker and CIO. The IT worker has the right to submit ideas about new product whereas the CIO shares the same right and also has the ability to accept ideas which could be implemented.

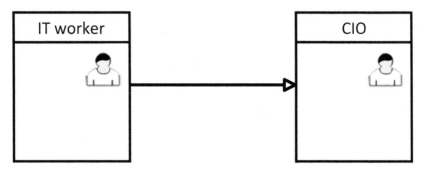

Figure 7: Generalization example

4 IT Support for Extended Conversation Diagrams

We are aware that a new or extended notation without an appropriate IT support (i.e. modeling tool) is pointless. To that end, we decided to prototypically implement xCD in existing modeling tools. We selected two commercial and one open-source modeling tool, all of which had the possibility of introducing new user-defined elements.

The first tool we selected was Microsoft Visio. It is a generic diagraming tool, which is part of the Microsoft Office software package (Helmers 2013). Visio offers the possibility of introducing user-defined elements in different ways and organizing them into stencils.

ARIS Business Architect is collaborative process design software (Davis & Brabander 2007). With this tool every user can simply design, analyze and administer a business process. It includes over 200 different business notations, such as BPMN, UML, ARIS, etc. It also includes two supporting tools: an element editor and a connection matrix editor, which are helpful when defining new elements and connections between them.

On the open source software landscape, we chose a tool for modeling BPMN process models called Yaoqiang BPMN Editor. The tool demonstrated good compliance with BPMN specification. However, the implementation of new elements were shown to be complex for users with a limited knowledge about software development and software modeling tools. Table 3 summarizes the modeling tools which were selected for implementation of xCD.

Table 3: Software comparison table

	Microsoft Visio 2010	ARIS Business Architect	Yaoqiang BPMN Editor
Basic information			
Company	Microsoft	Software AG	Open source community
Commercial / Open source	Commercial	Commercial	Open source
Desktop / Web application	Desktop	Desktop	Desktop
Generic / Dedicated software	Generic	Generic	Dedicated
BPMN 2.0			
Compliant with BPMN 2.0 specification	BPMN Visio Modeler plugin	Partially, connections are not included	Yes
On the list of BPMN 2.0 consistent software	Only plugin	Yes	No
BPMN 2.0 elements	Only in plugin	Yes	Yes
BPMN 2.0 connections	Only in plugin	Yes	Yes
Syntax validation	No	Yes	Only for business processes
Implementation			
User defined elements	JPG, PNG, own drawing	ARIS Symbol Editor	Yes, with symbols
User defined connections	Yes	Only like rules	No
Connection rules between elements	No	Yes, connection matrix	No
Export graphic package	Yes	No	No
Interoperability			
Import and export of user defined models (BPMN XML)	No	Yes	Yes
Other format to export models	PDF, JPG, PNG, AutoCad, etc.	PNG, JPG	PNG, JPG, BMP, GIF, SVG, VML, etc.

Through our research, we have come to a conclusion that the most applicable modeling tool for implementation of xCD is ARIS Business Architect. It is possible to precisely define an element and its visual attributes. An implementer can also precisely define connections between elements with the use of a connection matrix. The main disadvantage is its inability to validate connections between elements. ARIS Business Architect is also the only tool from our research that is on the OMG's BPMN list of complaint modeling tools.

The two other tools that were part of the investigation have the following principal advantages and disadvantages. Microsoft Visio has a commercial plugin which is consistent with BPMN 2.0 standard. On the other hand, it has problems with defining graphical connections between elements. The main advantage of Yaoqing BPMN Editor is its open source license, which extends the possibilities for tool reuse. However, it was shown to be inappropriate for implementing user-defined elements.

5 Discussion

Conversation diagrams, which were introduced in BPMN 2.0, are primarily used for modeling 'process landscapes' and basic interactions between different process participants. With the additional 15 new elements which were introduced in our research, we adapted conversation diagrams for modeling organizational communication including e-communication. The new elements were defined on three levels: conceptual, logical and physical, including an extended meta-model and serialization of all elements. Additionally, we implemented the extended notation into three modeling tools – Microsoft Visio, ARIS Business Architecture and Yaoqiang BPMN Editor.

As a preliminary, these new elements were compared with existing elements. This evaluation was performed by the first-year IT students who were unaware of conversation diagrams and their extensions and therefore offered a suitable population for identifying the benefits and weaknesses on both notations. Students perceived the existing notation as being faster for modeling and less error prone, mostly due to its simplicity. The extended notation was perceived as more understandable and suitable for modeling complex situations.

Based on these preliminary results, we want to continue with our research to improve the extended notation and afterwards to experimentally investigate if modelers would accept the proposed extensions to conversation diagrams.

References

Allweyer, T., 2010. *BPMN 2.0*, Norderstedt: BoD.

Chinosi, M. & Trombetta, A., 2011. *Result of the BPMN Usage Survey*. Available at: http://www.slideshare.net/mchinosi/bpmn-usage-survey-results.

Chinosi, M. & Trombetta, A., 2012. BPMN: An introduction to the standard. *Computer Standards & Interfaces*, 34(1), pp. 124–134.

Davis, R. & Brabander, E., 2007. *ARIS Design Platform: Getting Started with BPM*, Springer Science & Business Media.

Dumas, M., van der Aalst, W.M. & ter Hofstede, A.H., 2005. *Process-Aware Information Systems: Bridging People and Software Through Process Technology*, John Wiley & Sons.

Eloranta, L., Kallio, E. & Terho, I., 2006. A Notation Evaluation of BPMN and UML Activity Diagrams. *Special Course in Information Systems*.

Erl, T., 2005. *Service-Oriented Architecture: Concepts, Technology, and Design*, Upper Saddle River, NJ, USA: Prentice Hall PTR.

Helmers, S., 2013. *Microsoft Visio 2013 Step By Step*, 1st edn., Sebastopol, CA: Microsoft Press.

Husemann, B., Lechtenbörger, J. & Vossen, G., 2000. Conceptual Data Warehouse Design. In *Proc. of the International Workshop on Design and Management of Data Warehouses (DMDW 2000)*, pp. 3–9.

Larkin, J.H. & Simon, H.A., 1987. Why a Diagram Is (Sometimes) Worth Ten Thousand Words. *Cognitive Science*, 11(1), pp. 65–100.

Moody D.L., 2009. The „Physics" of Notations: Toward a Scientific Basis for Constructing Visual Notations in Software Engineering. *IEEE Transactions on Software Engineering*, 35(6), pp. 756–79.

OMG, 2011. Business Process Model and Notation version 2.0. Available at: http://www.omg.org/spec/BPMN/2.0/ [Accessed March 15, 2011].

Popper, K., 1978. "Three Worlds." Available at: http://tannerlectures.utah.edu/_documents/a-to-z/p/popper80.pdf.

Richmond, V.P. & McCroskey, J.C., 2008. *Organizational Communication for Survival: Making Work, Work*, 4th edn., Boston: Pearson.

Rumbaugh, J., Jacobson, I. & Booch, G., 2004. *The Unified Modeling Language Reference Manual*, 2nd edn., Pearson Higher Education.

Shapiro, R. et al., 2011. *BPMN 2.0 Handbook Second Edition: Methods, Concepts, Case Studies and Standards in Business Process Modeling Notation*, Future Strategies, Incorporated.

Turkalj, Z. & Fosic, I., 2009. "Organizational Communication as an Important Factor of Organizational Behaviour." *Interdisciplinary Management Research*, 5, pp. 33–42.

Nadja Damij and Dolores Modic
Faculty of Information Studies in Novo mesto, Slovenia

Remodeling the Preparation Phase of Intellectual Property Processes via an Activity Table

Abstract: Companies are faced with difficulties regarding the efficiency of their intellectual property, stemming from both the unsuitable choice of individual (formal or informal) protection mechanisms as well as their sub-optimal use. In this article we present a way in which the activity table technique may be a useful, comprehensive, holistic, but still relatively simple way for intellectual property protection processes' improvement; allowing us to find bottle-necks and ways to avoid them as well as include a systematic element into processes usually riddled by informality and accompanied by a high level of uncertainty. In doing this, we highlight the steps and considerations that are needed in order to be able to use the activity table.

Keywords: Intellectual property processes; activity table; process modeling; SMEs

1 Introduction

The focal idea of this paper is to model the activity table in order to increase the efficiency of intellectual property protection, while keeping in mind that small and mediums sized companies, and all those who do not engage in IP management to a significant extent, are especially susceptible to the issues intellectual property (IP) processes' management.

Throughout the last decades, the fields of business process modeling and consequently business process renovation have been gaining recognition and acceptance. Business processes come within our scope in that they potentially add value to the organization and as such are attracting attention (see the examples given in Aguilar-Saven 2003, Hammer & Champy 1993, and so forth). Consequently, business process modeling and improvement is on the increase, as only a thorough comprehension of the business processes within organizations can lead to effective, efficient and value-adding systems.

In the case of intellectual property (IP) protection processes, there is a high level of uncertainty. In general, uncertainties stem from incomplete or missing information, which makes it impossible to forecast future events, take informed decisions and retain (complete) control over results. Following Troy and Werle (2008) two types of uncertainties come to play: so-called fundamental uncertainty – referring to the lack of necessary information in the system as a whole – and the so-called strategic uncertainty, referring to the asymmetrical dispersion of necessary information. Inside IP processes tend to contribute to an unsuitable choice of (formal or informal) mechanisms as well as their sub-optimal use (see also Modic 2013). Today the revised strategies of patenting, and thereby the increase in strategic handling of intellectual property (Modic 2013, Neuheussler 2009, Blackburn 2007, Matthews, Pickering & Kirkland 2007), underline the rise of intellectual property applications. Many authors also claim that intellectual property rights may today be seen more as barriers to innovation by the competition than as an innovation enabler. To go beyond these critiques one must be aware of the different facets of intellectual property processes.

During the improvement of individual IP processes it is hence necessary for companies to be offered standardized (typical) processes and their individual elements, so they are able – taking into account the differences between them – to identify elements that are in need of improvement. One way in which to bring more stability and less uncertainty is quality IP creation (not having in mind the original "spark", but rather the continuation of the path to the stage of commercialization) and good IP management, which may provide a sufficient basis for the successful exploitation of the IP rights.

2 The Activity Table

The concept of the activity table was developed by Damij et al. (2008). The new element in the activity table is the inclusion of the property table parameters. As such, the activity table represents a complete process system.

In order to develop a process model that represents a true likeness of the existing reality of the process, the state of existing knowledge of the process should be first discovered and understood (Damij et al. 2008). The process model represented by the activity table is developed. This table consists of two parts. The first part provides information about each activity of the process by defining a number of parameters that describe the activities listed. The second part is a tabular-graphical representation of the process discussed. The activity table hence ensures that the presented process model is in fact a true likeness of the real-life business process. To develop the activity table, information about process functioning should be gained during interviews with knowledgeable employees. This is done using the following two steps: the activity parameters and the business processes.

In the columns of part 1 of the activity table, one or more of the following parameters are defined for each activity (i), where i ranges from 1 to the number of activities:

- Description. A short and precise description of what exactly is the work carried out by the activity defined in row (i) of the table.
- Time. The expected duration needed for activity (i) to be processed and accomplished.
- Rule. One or more constraints or rules that must be satisfied in order for activity (i) to be performed.
- Input/Ouput. Input(s) and output(s) of activity (i).
- Other parameters can be added if necessary.

The process modelling starts by identifying the behavior of the business processes identified. For each process, we create a new activity table, which represents its „as-is" model of the process. Thus, the name of the process selected is written in the first column of the activity table: see Table 1. If the process is large and complex, then it may be partitioned into a set of sub-processes, which are in this case listed in the second column of the activity table.

As previously mentioned, each process consists of a number of work processes, which are defined in the work process column of the activity table. This column is usually the second one in which all work processes of the process discussed are listed. In addition, for each work process defined, we write in the first row of the table the name of the department in which the work process is performed: see Table 1.

A work process is a process that consists of a set of activities performed within a certain department. To identify these activities, further interviews are organized with the employees of this department. An activity is a micro-process that represents well-defined work performed by one resource

(Damij & Damij 2014). For each work process listed in the work process column, we have to identify all activities that are performed within the framework of the work process discussed. These activities are listed in the activity column, which is usually the third column in the table. For each activity, we have to identify:

a) the resource that executes the activity, and indicate it in a certain column of the second row under the department in which the work process is defined; and
b) the predecessor and successor activities of the current activity, and connect it to these activities by vertical arrows.

Table 1: The activity table

# Process	Work Process	Activity	Parameters											
			Description	Time	Rule	Input/output								

The activity table technique uses a small set of flowchart symbols to model a process, such as: $\circ, \circledcirc, \square, \lozenge, |, \rightarrow, \leftarrow, \downarrow, \uparrow$. These symbols have the following meanings (Damij & Damij 2014):

- Symbol $\circ$ indicates the starting point of a process;
- Symbol $\circledcirc$ indicates the end point of a process or a certain path of the process;
- Symbol $\square$ in cell (i, j) of the table means that resource (j) performs activity (i), where j ranges from 1 to the number of resources and i ranges from 1 to the number of activities;
- Symbol $\lozenge$ in cell (i, j) means that activity (i) is a decision activity;
- Horizontal arrows $\rightarrow, \leftarrow$ are used to connect the activities horizontally;
- Vertical arrows $\downarrow, \uparrow$ are used to link the activities vertically;

- Symbol * in cell (i, j) and cell (i, k) mean that activity (i) could be performed by resource (j) or resource (k).

3 Remodeling the Preparation Phase of the Intellectual Property Processes with the Help of the Activity Table

In the IP protection (preparation) process we can see three steps: processes that are related to the identification; those related to the selection; and those related to the registration (if needed). Let us now depict the standardized (model) processes and other characteristics of the activity table. These standardized (model) processes help companies to identify the inefficiencies of existing processes while using the activity table in order to remodel and improve the processes of intellectual property protection.

In order to use the activity table, next, the model parameters need to be defined: business process, work processes and defining activities and activity parameters (description, time, rule, input/output). To develop the activity table in the field of IP protection, information about process functioning should be gained during interviews with knowledgeable employees. These are especially (but not exclusively) innovators, R&D department heads, marketing and/or sales department employees, the finance and management/directors, the legal department and/or patent attorney (if existing). There tends however to be a lack of IP protection-related knowledge, which would seem to suggest the advisability of including an even wider variety of respondents (this also goes hand in hand with the general innovation directions, aspiring to involve as many employees as possible in innovation processes).

The business process is the intellectual property protection process in its narrower sense. The processes are related to three steps: those related to the identification, those related to the selection and those related to the registration (if needed). The preparation process in general includes six work processes: identification of appropriate innovation, identification of protection goals, identification of existing protection mechanisms, selection of the exploitation mode, selection of protection mechanisms and registration or non-registration formation.

The identification of appropriate innovation includes the following: collecting the innovations, the identification of characteristics of innovations, the identification of market needs, the identification of active/not active IP protection and, possibly, the making of the prototype. The first activity may be organized in several different fashions: weekly staff meetings, innovation forms, "innovation black-boxes" etc.; the second can be organized as a meeting; and the third as a written analysis/statement of market potential. Next, we have the possible making of the prototype (by the inventor and/ or R&D department or an external actor altogether). It is to be noted that for the IP protection processes, the viability of the innovation is pro forma practically unimportant; however from the point of view of making a profit, it is of utmost importance. Furthermore the decision to pursue active protection is done as a written or oral statement. Lastly, we have the agreement with the inventor(s) to take over a work-related innovation; this should take place at the very beginning to avoid any future problems. Involved employees are hence the innovator(s) and the R&D head (also possible: an innovation commission), marketing and sales department employees; the legal department; and a management representative: in other words, those included in the innovation identification team. The outputs are description of the innovation (preferably on a form), a short market and sales analysis/ statement, the decision to actively pursue/not pursue active protection, and a working prototype (relevant for technological innovations). The latter is also followed by the decision to take over the work-related innovation and the possible signing of a non-disclosure agreement.

The work process of protection goals identification includes the identification of strategic goals related to intellectual property protection processes in general, and the definition of specific goals. This involves the innovator(s), the management representative, legal department, sales department representatives (in other words, the strategic team). The outputs are (at minimum) a devised strategy for IP protection and a statement on specific goals for the selected innovation. Next, the process for the identification of existing protection mechanisms includes an analysis of potential protection mechanisms (both formal as well as informal) and devising the viability of individual protection mechanisms. Involved employees are the innovator or R&D head, management representative, financial department and the legal department. The outputs are an analysis of potential (viable) protection mechanisms and a viability study/statement of individual protection mechanisms.

Selection of the exploitation mode involves reaching a decision on the exploitation mode (goods market, IP market, strategic use), since the next steps are also dependent on this decision. The selection of should include the participation of the innovator as well as the R&D department head, sales department head and management head. The output is the decision as to the mode of exploitation.

The work process of the selection of protection mechanisms encompasses the decision to use a specific formal or informal protection mechanism; relevant considerations are the characteristics of the innovation, the goal of intellectual property protection, the cost and available funds, competition, and the desired timeframe. The decision must also be made on a further level: which sub-possibility of a certain protection mechanism should be used (for example: to apply for a national, European or PCT patent). Involved employees are the management, the legal department and perhaps also the patent attorney. Further advice may be sought from competition (if suitable links are established). Outputs are: the decision on the selection of the protection mechanism and a rewritten (in light of the above) draft of innovation characteristics.

We are faced with distinct activities dependent on whether we have chosen protection via formal or via informal mechanisms: that is, either to use a registration procedure or not. In the first case those involved in this step depend on whether there is cooperation with an (outside) patent attorney or if the company is preparing the application on its own. The first presumes the active participation of the patent attorney, the other the active participation of either the legal department (if existing) or the management. The activities involve: turning the draft into the application (in the case of formal IPRs) (and for an international/foreign application the translation(s) of the application (or part of the application) to the requisite languages is also required); sending the application to the IP office; communication with the IP office; possible corrections demanded by the IP office; and payment of the registration fee(s). Even for non-formal protection mechanisms, some steps need to be taken. For example, in the case of trade secrets, although the mechanism is often depicted as an informal one, several demands need to be met in order to be legally-protected trade secrets. (These often vary between countries, but usually include provisions about the definition of data included in company documents and provisions about physical treatment of documents containing sensitive data about individual innovation.)

Due to the lack of relevant knowledge on IP, we see it as important to at least offer an outline of model IP protection processes, allowing easier potential use of the activity table.

Table 2: Identifying the appropriate innovation in the preparation phase

Business process	Work process	Activity	Parameters				Department/team R&D department Employees			Department/team Sales marketing departments Employees		Department/team Management legal departments Employees		
			Description	Time	Rule	Input/output	Innovator	R&D dep. head	R&D team	Marketing employee	Sales employee	R&D director	General director	Employ Legal dept.
IP protection (preparation) process	Identification of appropriate innovation	Collecting the innovations	Overview of innovations forms	10 min	No suggestions	Description of the innovations collected								
		Identification of characteristics of the innovations	Analysis of innovation forms meeting	1h	Lack of needed knowledge	Innovation characteristics identified								
		Market needs identification	Preliminary analysis of market potential	1h	Lack of data on market potential	Written analysis statement of market potential								
		Making of the prototype	Prototype construction or innovation viability check	n.a.	Prototype not viable	Prototype or viability check								
		Identification of active/not active IP protection	Decision-making whether to pursue or not pursue active IP protection	15 min	No agreement	Written or oral statement								
		Decision to take over the innovation	Decision-making and agreement with the inventor to take over or not to take over the invention	1 week	No consent from the inventor	Written statement, written & signed agreement with the inventor								

Table 2 shows a possible outline of the activity table for the work process of innovation identification. The next step would be to insert into the flowchart the set of flowchart symbols defined above in order to model the process. There are no significant deviations from the above-suggested flowchart symbols. Once this is done, the flowchart allows us to see bottle-necks and inconsistencies, by analyzing the individual parts of the flowchart, taking into account the suggestions and comments made in this article, as well as by consulting other literature or existing good practices.

4 Conclusion

Innovation and entrepreneurship are tightly interconnected, since for companies the final desired outcome is profit. Therefore, to achieve this outcome, it is necessary that innovation be organized as a systematic activity (Drucker 2010, p. xv). This is especially true for intellectual property protection processes, which are laced with uncertainties and lack of knowledge.

In this article we propose the activity table technique as a tool, one which is, in our opinion, especially valuable for small and medium sized companies as well as those actors who do not deal with their IP processes in great depth but who seek a simple and manageable tool to help them remodel their IP processes in order to enhance their efficiency.

Acknowledgments

This work is supported by Creative Core FISNM-3330-13-500033 'Simulations' project funded by the European Union, the European Regional Development Fund. The operation is carried out within the framework of the Operational Programme for Strengthening Regional Development Potentials for the period 2007–2013, Development Priority 1: Competitiveness and Research Excellence, Priority Guideline 1.1: Improving the Competitive Skills and Research Excellence.

References

Aguilar-Saven, Ruth Sara: "Business Process Modelling: Review and Framework." *International Journal of Production Economics* 90(2), 2003, pp. 129–149.

Blackburn, Robert A: *Intellectual Property and Innovation Management in Small Firms.* Routledge: London, New York 2007.

Damij Nadja / Damij Talib: *Process Management. A Multi-disciplinary Guide to Theory, Modeling, and Methodology.* Springer-Verlag: Berlin, Heidelberg 2014.

Damij Nadja, Damij Talib / Grad, Janez / Jelenc Franc: "A Methodology for Business Process Improvement and IS Development." *Inf. Softw. Technol.* 50, 2008, pp. 1127–1141.

Drucker, Peter F.: *Innovation and Entrepreneurship.* Elsevier: Oxford and Burlington 2010.

Hammer, Michael / Champy, James: *Re-Engineering the Corporation: A Manifesto for Business Revolution.* Harper Business: New York 1993.

Matthews, Duncan / Pickering John / Kirkland, John: "A Strategic Approach to Managing Intellectual Property." In R.A Blackburn, (ed.), *Intellectual Property and Innovation Management in Small Firms.* Routledge: London, New York 2007, pp. 35–54.

Modic, Dolores: *Novi vidiki intelektualne lastnine v kontekstu inovacijskih sistemov (na primeru Slovenije)* [New Views on Intellectual Property Protection in the Context of Innovation Systems (in the case of Slovenia)]. Doctoral thesis. FUDŠ: Nova Gorica 2013.

Neuheusler, Peter: "Formal vs. Informal Protection Instruments and the Strategic Use of Patents in an Expected-Utility Framework." In Peter Neuheusler (ed.), *Innovation Systems and Policy Analysis* (Fraunhofer ISI Discussion Papers No. 20). Fraunhofer Institute for Systems and Innovation Research: Karlsruhe 2009, pp. 1–28.

Troy, Irene / Werle, Raymund: "Uncertainty and Market for Patents." *MPIfG Working Paper 08/2.* Max Plank Institute for the Study of Societies: Koeln 2008, pp. 1–24.

www.ingramcontent.com/pod-product-compliance
Lightning Source LLC
La Vergne TN
LVHW022323060326
832902LV00020B/3630